WHAT'S HAPPENING
TO OUR CHILDREN?

Anthony Bullen, from 1964 to 1975, was
Director of Religious Education for the
Archdiocese of Liverpool, England. As
Director he was responsible for a programme
of religious studies for children from Kinder-
garten to High School – a programme in use
in many parts of the world. He is the author
of a number of books for religious teachers
and activity-booklets for children. During
the last decade he has been in constant dialogue with parents, teachers and children
over the subject of religious education. He
is now pastor of a busy parish in Liverpool.

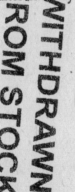

by the same author

Living for God

Growing in Christ

Exploring God's World:
a religious programme for infants

Living and Believing:
a religious programme for 8-11-year-olds

Growing Christian (Books I-IV)

Twenty-Four Assemblies for Juniors

Catholic Prayer Book

Praying the Mass

also in Fontana Books

Companion to the Good News
(With Joseph Rhymer)

Parents, Children and God

ANTHONY BULLEN

What's Happening to Our Children?

Faith - tensions in
Christian Families Today

Collins

FONTANA BOOKS

First published by Fontana Books 1974
Second Impression November 1974
Third Impression April 1975
Fourth Impression August 1977

© Anthony Bullen 1974

Made and printed in Great Britain by
William Collins Sons & Co Ltd Glasgow

'. . . the future of humanity
lies in the hands of those who are strong enough
to provide coming generations
with reasons for living and hoping.'

(Vatican II)

This book is dedicated
to those Christians
who believe they are weak
but who really are strong
because they are open to the power of God.

Acknowledgements

The author and publishers wish to acknowledge their indebtedness for permission to reproduce copyright material as follows:

from *Between Parent and Child* by Dr Haim G. Ginott (Staples Press Ltd.); from *The Christian Century* (issue 7 May 1969) poem by Jeanette Hind; from *Christian Involvement* by Bernard Cooke (Argus Communications) reprinted with permission of Argus Communications, Niles, Illinois from *For All Men* by J. B. Walker (Darton, Longman & Todd Ltd.); from *In the Redeeming Christ* by F. X. Durrwell (Sheed & Ward Ltd.) from *It Is the Lord* by William Bausch (Fides Publishers); from *Jesus Christ Superstar* by Tim Rice (Leeds Music); from *Life for a Wanderer* by Andrew Greeley (Image Books); from *A New Catechism* (Search Press Ltd.); from *On Becoming a Person* by Carl Rogers (Constable & Co. Ltd.) from *Prayer in the Secular City* by Douglas Rhymes (Lutterworth Press); from *School for Prayer* by Archbishop Bloom (Darton, Longman & Todd Ltd.); from *Step by Step* (Motherwell Religious Education Centre); from *Your Word Is Near* by Huub Oosterhuis (Newman Press) reprinted with permission of Newman Press. Copyright © 1968 by The Missionary Society of St Paul the Apostle in the State of New York.

The author wishes to thank the BBC and Beryl's husband for permission to reproduce Roy Trevivian's interview with Beryl.

The quotations from the New Testament are mainly from *Good News for Modern Man* (Fontana).

The illustrations are by Denis Waugh.

Contents

A Letter to the Reader

Dear Reader,

Since I wrote *Parents, Children and God* some years ago, various people have said to me, 'Well, it wasn't too bad as far as it went. But don't you think you ought to write a follow-up to it?' Eventually I became ashamed of making excuses, and was forced to start work on a sequel.

In writing *What's Happening to Our Children?* I have had in mind the people (parents and teachers) who first read *Parents, Children and God*, but as they are now, that is, a few years on. They are doubtless feeling a little older and a little more puzzled at the way in which their more sophisticated children look at religion and life. I ought to say immediately that *What's Happening to Our Children?* offers no slick solutions, no ready-made answers to the problems facing Christian families today. Rather it attempts to lead the reader into a re-examination of his own understanding of the Faith, a reappraisal of his own relationship with God through Jesus Christ. This, I believe, is the only way in which the gap between growing children and their parents can be bridged.

A word of warning: kind friends who have read this book in typescript tell me that chapters 2, 3, 4 and 5 are rather heavy going. They suggested that I might put these chapters at the end of the book. I carefully considered their advice but finally decided not to act on it. I believe that although this section may be hard going, it needs to be read at the beginning. So I ask you not to put the book aside if you find this part difficult. I think you will find chapter 6 and subsequent chapters not only much easier but also making more sense once you have become familiar with the earlier chapters.

Finally, if I may be allowed a military comparison: I have no doubt that a private in the Army Education Corps is not grudging in his admiration for the fearless front-liner in the bomb-disposal squad who calmly defuses the most lethal devices with only seconds to go. While not implying that teenage boys and girls may be compared to time-bombs, the simile nevertheless expresses something of the admiration the author feels towards the men and women of today who, despite being Christian parents and teachers in the 1970s, still manage to keep their cool.

With sincere regards,
Anthony Bullen

Liverpool
14 August 1973

CHAPTER I

Puzzled Parents

'It makes us wonder where we went wrong. We sent him to the best school. We gave him everything he wanted. Yes, and plenty of affection too. He appeared to love and trust us. And we trusted him – perhaps too much. Within a year of his going to university, we discovered, almost by accident, that he was mixing with a most undesirable lot of students. On his first summer vacation he told us he wouldn't be coming to church with us any more. Mind you, he was very polite about it. "I don't want to hurt your feelings," he said, "but I can't believe any longer in all that religious stuff they gave me at school. And please don't think that this is just a phase and I'll eventually grow out of it. Because I shan't."

'At first we tried to remonstrate with him. But in the end we gave up; we had to. He said, "If you mention religion just once more I'll go round this house and smash up everything breakable." '

There has always been a 'generation gap'. From earliest times, middle-aged parents have complained of their unruly sons and daughters. But now the gap seems surely wider than ever. The youngsters, whom older people claim they cannot understand, are children of a breed very different from their elders. Some people call them 'TV children' – children who have been born and grown up alongside the television set. But they are also 'Atomic Age' children: they have known no other existence than that of a life lived with the threat of instantaneous global annihilation without warning. They are born in an age of rapid change, which is bound to affect their stability. They are 'Space Age' children who a few years ago may have been less surprised than their elders at the first 'giant step' for mankind taken by Neil Armstrong as he walked on the moon. (I remember that Sunday in July well. I was attending a social for school-leavers. The other teachers and I crept away to the TV room unable to resist the temptation to watch the dramatic pictures live from the moon. The youngsters carried on dancing!)

Parents of today could claim that their offspring of 15-25 years of age have grown up in an era of greater scientific and technological advancement than any other throughout the whole previous history of mankind.

IDEAS IN THE AIR

Nor have they escaped, even the most sheltered of them, from being influenced by the prevailing philosophies. The existentialism of modern philosophy has coloured very many television programmes. (One does not need to know what existentialism means to have been affected by this view of life.) Agnostic secularism has made it that a 'world come of age' no longer needs God to supply solutions to the few questions left unanswered. The 'God of the gaps' – the God who used to be invited to step forward when no other explanation could be found to solve an inexplicable event – that God is dead for most of our youngsters. Those who still believe in God are more likely to say 'God needs us' than 'we need God'. Or, as one of the characters in Leonard Bernstein's *Mass* sings in the Credo, 'I'd believe in twenty Gods if they'd believe in me.'

Middle-aged parents may look nostalgically back to a

time when the voice of authority was unquestionably accepted.

'We would never have dared to ask "why?" of our parents or teachers. Nor would we have presumed to have queried the doctrines put before us by the Church. Of course, we may have had secret doubts. We may have rebelled "inside", but for most of us, well, we just accepted things as they were and took it for granted that if those in authority insisted on the truth of various statements or the rightness of various actions then we should accept them without question. But nowadays — one constantly hears these young ones querying the right of older and so wiser people to tell them what is true or false, right or wrong.'

It's certainly true that young people of today are much more concerned with asking 'why?' than were their parents. But is this altogether a bad thing? An important book to emerge from the last war was Victor Frankl's *Man's Search for Meaning*. Professor Frankl, using the death camps (of which he was an inmate) as a lurid back-cloth, points to the moral: those who survived the concentration camps were those who had found meaning to their lives. And how else had they come to accept meaning in their lives but by constantly asking that very question 'why'? It would be wrong to think that questioning the meaning of beliefs and rituals, patterns of behaviour and social practices is necessarily a sign of disbelief or rebellion.

BACKWARDS INTO THE FUTURE

If the difference between the younger people of today and their elders is so pronounced, is it any wonder that there are today so many puzzled parents, and puzzled Christian parents?

The purpose of this book is to help young and old look at themselves and at each other, at their beliefs and disbeliefs, neither to denounce nor necessarily to discard. Rather it is to help the young see that the present is built on the past, to convince the older generation that change is not necessarily bad. A modern philosopher has said, 'We walk backwards into the future.' This could be the motto for the older generation. Could the younger invert this to read, 'We walk forwards into the future but we are looking over our shoulders into the past'?

CONCLUSIONS OF A LIFE-TIME

All of us need to look again at our beliefs. This book attempts to light up certain areas which the author believes are crucial to an authentic understanding of the Good News today. If the chasm between the generations is to be narrowed then honest, open-minded discussion must be allowed. We must learn the difficult art of listening to each other. That great psychotherapist, Carl Rogers, in a remarkable essay sums up three of his findings of a life-time as follows:

I have found it of enormous value when I can permit myself to understand another person.

I have found it enriching to open channels whereby others can communicate their feelings, their private conceptual worlds, to me.

I have found it highly rewarding when I can accept another person.[1]

DISCOVERING THE TRUTH

This book may, of course, simply be read. But at the back of the author's mind during the time he has been writing it has been the hope that it will be used rather

[1] *On Becoming a Person* (Constable and Co. Ltd., 1962).

as a discussion booklet, a springboard for a friendly interchange of experience, opinion, belief. Each member of the group brings with him his own experience, background, and level of maturity. He learns not only by listening to the other members of the group, but also by giving verbal expression to his own understanding of life and religion. This interplay of viewpoints almost always brings to light truths which the individual may never have discovered on his own. And to discover the truth has a more lasting effect than merely to accept it. 'Truth which is told is soon forgotten. Truth which is discovered lasts a life-time.' If we discuss openly with others, prepared all the time to try to appreciate – not necessarily agree with – their point of view, we cannot but benefit ourselves as persons.

'Real communication occurs . . . when we listen with understanding,' writes Carl Rogers.[2] 'What does this mean? It means to see the expressed idea and attitude from the other person's point of view. Stated so briefly, this may sound absurdly simple, but it is not . . . Some of you may be feeling that you listen well to people . . . the chances are that your listening has not been of the type I have described.' Rogers goes on to describe what he calls a little experiment to test the quality of listening.

The next time you get into an argument . . . with a small group of friends, just stop the discussion for a moment and institute this rule. 'Each person can speak up for himself only *after* he has first restated the ideas and feelings of the previous speaker accurately, and to that speaker's satisfaction.' You see what this would mean. It would simply mean that before presenting your own point of view, it would be necessary for you to really achieve the other per-

[2] Op. cit. pp. 331 ff.

son's frame of reference – to understand his thought and feelings so well that you could summarize them for him. Sounds simple, doesn't it? But if you try it, you will discover it is one of the most difficult things you have ever tried to do. However, once you have been able to see the other person's point of view, your own comments will have to be drastically revised. You will also find the emotion going out of the discussion, the differences being reduced, and those differences which remain being of a rational and understandable sort.

HOW TO CONDUCT A GROUP DISCUSSION

'All real living consists in meeting', in accepting other people – in sifting – not necessarily agreeing with – their views, and certainly in sharing their understanding of life and of faith. The value of discussion groups can hardly be doubted. If, then, this booklet is to be used for group discussion, it might be helpful to offer a few guidelines:

Six to eight members seems to be the best number for a group.

A chairman (or chairwoman) should lead the discussion. A different member of the group might be chairman at each meeting.

The meeting must start promptly at the time arranged. The meeting should last no more than one and a half hours. Ideally, the members should have the feeling at the end of the meeting that they would like it to have lasted longer.

Members should have studied a chapter of the book beforehand.

At the meeting they must be prepared to learn from each other – no one has a monopoly of the truth – and be prepared also to share their understanding and experience with each other. So the chairman should try on the one hand not to let anyone (including himself) take the lion's share of the discussion; on the other hand, he should try to encourage those members of the group who, perhaps, through shyness, are inclined to be 'passengers'.

After each member has had an opportunity to express his or her reaction to the chapter, the questions must be tackled. Almost all these questions appeal to the experience and opinions of the group. Few questions have only one correct answer.

If there is to be reporting back to a general meeting, a secretary should be appointed who will try to make a brief account of the meeting and its conclusions, if there should be any.

At the end of the meeting, two or three minutes should be allowed for silent prayer. As the group get to know each other better, individual members may care to make short spontaneous prayers related to the topic discussed.

CHAPTER 2

Let's Be Honest about God

'I came to this meeting for parents tonight because I wanted to discover how to help my child. Now you've come to the end of your talk, you ask if we have any questions.

'For years now I've looked on my religion just as a collection of rules I obey, practices I practise, beliefs I believe in. I go to church most Sundays. I say my prayers, morning and night. I've never had any great joy in my religion. Nor has it ever made any great demands on me. I've just plodded on from day to day doing the various things I've been supposed to do.

'Now, tonight, you say religion is meant to be much more than that. You say it's a life to be lived, a living and loving relationship with the Father, with the Son, with the Spirit. It's the first time I've ever thought of it in this way.

'I don't mind admitting that I've never really bothered very much with the Father or the Spirit. Of course I've prayed the "Our Father", and I've also given a nod in the direction of the Holy Spirit on Whit Sunday. But other than that, I've got by with just our Lord. I must say I'm interested in what you have said. It seems to me to offer a fuller religious life than the narrow one I have been leading.

'My question is this: I don't seem to have an awareness of this living relationship with God (or should I say with Father, Son and Spirit?). I should like to be aware of it. How do I set about getting it?'

How should one answer such a question as this?
Before sketching the lines on which one might suggest
an answer, it may be helpful if we just look again at our
idea of God – leaving on one side for the moment, the
doctrine of the three Persons in God – the Trinity.

OLD MAN IN THE SKY

We may, in the course of years, try to refine the idea
of God we first received when we were very young, but
we never totally succeed. Deep down inside most of us,
if we admit the truth, there still remains the image of
an old man in the sky. If we strip away the alterations
which we have painted for ourselves over the years in
our attempt at projecting a more adult portrait of God,
underneath we can still see the faded remnants of this
picture of a grandfatherly figure. A benign figure most
of the time, slightly annoyed some of the time (when
we sin slightly), really angry at other times (when we
sin gravely).

It's not insignificant that when children are asked,
'What's your idea of God?' however else their descrip-
tions vary, nearly always they include the notion that
'he has a beard'. A questionnaire sent to a group of
thirteen-year-olds included: 'What three questions
would you like to ask God?', and in their replies one
has an insight into the somewhat grotesque image many
youngsters have:

How old are you?
Who made you?
What year were you born?
Where did you come from?
Are you real?
Would you like to get married?

One boy answered, perhaps very honestly, 'If I met God,
I wouldn't have the guts to ask him any questions.'

MAKING GOD IN OUR IMAGE

'God made man in his own image and likeness,' we read in the first book of the Bible. But is it not possible that all of us to some extent are guilty of making God in our image? J. B. Phillips[1] suggests a list of false images, some of which he believes are worshipped by most of us.

One false image is that for some 'God is a Resident Policeman.' He is equated with conscience or, more precisely, with a guilty conscience. 'It is extremely unlikely that we shall ever be moved to worship, love, and serve, a nagging inner voice that at worst spoils our pleasure and at best keeps us rather negatively on the path of virtue.'

Another false image of God is the 'Grand Old Man' — a 'great power in his day, but who could not possibly be expected to keep pace with modern progress'. (A pupil suggested as one of the questions he would like to ask God, 'What were things like in your day?' The implication is obvious: 'Your day is over.' To all intents and purposes, God is dead.)

Other false images which Canon Phillips lists are: 'God-in-a-box' (for the Anglo- or Roman Catholic, God is a Catholic, for the Low Church man, God hates incense and candles); the 'Managing Director' — 'Because he is in charge of so many people, he cannot possibly be aware of little me.'

It is easy, of course, to describe some of the misconceptions we all have about God. No great difficulty in saying what God *is not*; it's another matter altogether to attempt to say what God *is*. Even, however, allowing for that, we have to be unceasingly refining and revising our idea of God. We have continually to confess that our current image of God falls very far short of reality.

[1] *Your God is Too Small* (Epworth Press, 1952).

I held within myself the God, which I had made,
Dear graven image within my mind
And guarded close by every subtle kind
Of shield against attacks, which, hostile, laid
Against the truth, my truth, which could not fade,
From definitions clear within the rind
Impregnable to all attempts to find
A chink through which to thrust a spear of doubt.

Now you are here destructive of my peace
Whose doubt unbuilds the fortress of my mind
And hews my armoured framework piece by piece
Until I totter naked and in pain,
Uncertain . . . till I know that I am free
To soar to God, the God not made by me.'[2]

BEYOND OUR COMPREHENSION

Once we admit that God is beyond our comprehension, we are on the right lines. When we can say, 'O God, I worship you, even though I believe you are far different and far greater than the idea I have of you,' then our prayer is becoming more genuine. The realization that we are worshipping Someone than whom there is no one more beautiful, this realization develops our human personality and potential. Of course, we do not worship for that reason, simply to improve ourselves. It is rather that our awareness of the very magnificence of God elicits the desire to worship. And the very fact that we worship adds depth to our vision of life, broadens our horizons. This deepening and broadening process will, however, not come about if the God we worship is still the God of the five- or six-year-old child. A childish God. A petty God. To worship such a God does not elevate or ennoble a person. It may, in

[2] From a poem by Fr Finbar, quoted in the *Tablet*.

fact, enslave him. We must never allow ourselves to be satisfied with our present image of God. We must admit constantly to ourselves that our present understanding of God falls far short of the reality and that it always will.

'So far you haven't really answered my question. You have been speaking about "God". When you say "God" who are you talking about – the Father, the Son or the Spirit? Or all three? Is the living relationship I should have with God, really three relationships: one relationship with the Father, another with the Son, a third with the Spirit?'

In the preceding paragraph, it would have been more correct for me to have used the word 'Godhead' rather than 'God'. 'Godhead' really includes the three Persons of the Trinity. 'God' normally refers to the Father. This is the way the Bible uses the word 'God'. This is the presumption the Christian Church makes in its prayers: that when we say 'God', we mean 'the Father'. Of course Jesus is divine, truly equal to, but distinct from the Father. As also is the Spirit. But when I say 'Jesus is God', I am not saying 'Jesus is the Father.' This would not be true. Jesus said, 'The Father and I are one.' He did not say 'The Father and I are one and the same.'

PERSONS AND PEOPLE
Nor are we using the word 'Person' in the usual sense. This is not the place for a discussion on the way we understand 'Person' in respect of the Trinity. Sufficient for the moment if we keep in mind that the word 'Person' is applied to the three Persons of the Trinity in a way quite dissimilar to the manner in which we speak of ourselves as 'persons'. When we speak of the Trinity

we are not speaking about three separate people.

It is difficult to keep in mind at the same time both the oneness of God and the distinction of persons.

But the doctrine of the Trinity is not proposed to us simply as a matter for belief – a puzzle to test our faith. Jesus Christ revealed that the Godhead is so utterly Personal, that it demands to be comprised of three Persons. This he revealed not just for our assent in faith but so that we might enter into a relationship with each Person; real sons and daughters of a real Father. Real brothers and sisters of a real Brother. Real dependents on a real Advocate and Friend. If this appears to disunite the Trinity, then we might put it another way; we are children of God our Father because we are brothers (sisters) of Jesus, to whom we are united by the Spirit.

THE GOAL

The goal of our life's journey is the Father. Just as water must all the time travel towards the sea, so we are moving towards the goal of our life, the Father. While the water moves, it is attractive, picturesque, refreshing. When it stops moving towards the sea, it forms stagnant pools. When we resist the impulse to move towards the goal of our life, we become to some extent, dehumanized and depersonalized.

To change the simile: we are on a journey to our Father. He is not only the fount and source of life; He is the goal, the home-base, towards whom we are travelling. Accompanying us on our journey homewards is Jesus Christ, God-with-us, Emmanuel. He too has travelled the road that we are taking. And just as a man is drawn home by the spirit of homesickness, so too we, in our journey God-wards, are drawn by the Spirit of God.

'*You will pardon my saying so, but you still haven't answered my final question. I am not conscious of having this living relationship with Father, Son and Spirit. I should like it. How do I get it?*'

At the risk of appearing to duck your question, we had better leave the answering of it either to yourself or, better still, to the discussion group.

For discussion

1. Do we still have the same idea of God now as we had ten years ago?

2. Do you think that when youngsters say 'I don't believe in God any more' it is really an image of God they have outgrown which they don't believe in?

3. If we ask ourselves honestly what difference does the Trinity make to our lives, what answer do we give? Why is it wrong to say we can 'get by with just our Lord'?

4. Some people have said they have been put off the Trinity by pictorial representations. Old men with beards, doves for the Spirit, triangles, shamrocks, etc. Is this the group's experience?

5. How would you answer the questioner who wants an awareness of this living relationship with Father, Son and Spirit? What are the indications of a living relationship? (To help the answering of this question, contrast the qualities and interactions of husband and wife in a marriage that has died with those of a marriage that is happily alive.)

CHAPTER 3

Jesus Christ – Superstar or Saviour?

'That was quite a good take-off, wasn't it?'

'Yes. I'm always relieved when they say you can start smoking again.'

'If you look down now, you can see the coastline. Up there to the north is Galilee. Jerusalem is behind us on the other side.'

'You know your geography.'

'Well, I can see you are British. Was it your first visit to Israel?'

'Yes. But it was more of a visit to the Holy Land than to Israel, if you see what I mean.'

'You are a believing Christian then?'

'That's right. I was on a pilgrimage.'

'I'm Jewish myself. Not that I believe in the Jewish religion. I really don't believe in anything. I haven't got much time for faith.'

'I hope you won't mind my saying so, but that's nonsense. Almost everything you've done today depended on faith. You believed the taxi driver when he said he would take you to the airport. You believed the booking-in clerk when she told you when and where you would be called for the flight. You believe that the pilot is going to take you to London. Almost everything that happens to you in the next 24 hours is going to depend on faith in other people. So don't tell me you haven't got much time for faith. Life would just come to a halt if we didn't have faith.'

'But I'm talking about religious faith.'

'*So am I.*'

'*Well, tell me about your faith. You believe in Jesus Christ? I know virtually nothing about him even though he was a Jew.*'

'*He is a Jew.*'

'*But you can't speak about a dead man in the present tense.*'

'*I don't believe he's dead. He's alive.*'

'*You mean, you believe in his resurrection?*'

'*Exactly.*'

'*We have half an hour or so before they bring us lunch. Would you care to tell me what you believe about him?*'

Each Christian has his own faith-image of Jesus Christ. To be asked the question, 'Tell me what you believe about him' may be difficult to answer off the cuff, but it certainly helps one to reappraise the personal picture one has of Jesus. As with our understanding of God, our vision of Jesus, the Son of God, needs constantly to be revised, reappraised. It's not that what we thought of him, say, ten years ago, is now wrong. We simply see that our image of him then was less adequate than the one we have of him today. A wife, asked in the late 1970s to describe her husband and what he means to her, will give a different account from the one she would have given in the 1960s. The ten years will have seen a deepening relationship between them and the deepening relationship will have produced a deepening understanding. This is the 'mystery' of their marriage. And so it is or should be with the 'mystery of Jesus Christ'. If we have a relationship with him, it won't stand still. If our image of him has hardly altered over the years, then it probably means that our relationship with him is superficial.

GOD'S BEST GIFT TO MEN

God our Father has always loved men – not a love for a global humanity, but men and women individually. He loves you and me by name. His own Son was destined to be the supreme man, the model for all. It was because of him, for him, and by him, that creation thousands of millions of years ago gave the first push to the evolutionary process. Jesus was to be the highpoint of our universe. His coming into the world of creation was not just an afterthought, a repair job when things began to go wrong.

Christ is the visible likeness of the invisible God. He is the first-born Son, superior to all created things. For by him God created everything in heaven and on earth ... God created the whole universe through him and for him. (Colossians 1:15-16)

The coming of God's Son was not dependent upon the sin of men. The fact that from the beginning humans turned selfishly away from God (original sin) and so started a chain-reaction of sin, this made it that when he did come, he was not just the supreme human masterpiece of God, a model: he came also as a Saviour.

WHAT DID HE KNOW?

For thirty years he lived in a poor home, apparently indistinguishable from the other boys of Nazareth. When Mary called for him by name from the door of their cottage, more than one little boy would look up in the street: Jesus was a popular name.

What did he know of the future? There is a famous picture of the boy Jesus stretching his arms wide. In one hand is a hammer; in the other, nails. The shadow of the sunlight forms a cross behind him. The artist's intention is evident: from the beginning the manner of his death was clear to him. Can we really believe this?

Echoing the Epistle to the Hebrews, the fourth Eucharistic prayer describes Jesus as 'a man like us in all things but sin'. Could he have been a man like us in all things if he had known the future in detail? Surely, the most characteristic part of being a man is the painful process of groping, of searching, for an answer. 'It's only human.' How unlike a man (more like an automaton), if he had known all the answers! How could he have been truly free (and we speak of his death as 'a death he freely accepted'), if he had known all the circumstances of his later life before they had taken place? He would have been guilty of that most undesirable of characteristics, 'putting on an act', if, having known, he pretended that he hadn't. God the Son became truly man – but he brought no ready-made scenario from heaven with him.[1]

ONE OF US

It is as important to bring home to ourselves the true humanness of Jesus as it is to remind ourselves of his divinity. We can come to believe in his divinity only after we are convinced of his humanity. (cf. *General Catechetical Directory*, par. 53.) The questionnaire referred to in a previous chapter included a section devoted to the pupils' understanding of Jesus Christ. 'What would you like most to know about Jesus?' The most frequent response from these young people was:

Did Jesus ever exist?

Was Jesus real?

[1] This is not the place to enter into discussion about his predictions of his Passion, his prophecy of the destruction of Jerusalem, and the extraordinary knowledge of certain events (e.g. Lazarus' death) as attributed to him by the Fourth Evangelist. Readers who would like to pursue this question further, and also the more sensitive question of his self-awareness, are referred to *Jesus, God and Man* by Raymond E. Brown (Geoffrey Chapman, 1968).

Is he just a story?
Was he a ghost or was he a man?
Did he ever think of getting married?
Jesus, I think you are too good to be true.

These youngsters wanted to be convinced that he was a real man, not because they wanted to deny his divinity, but so that they could believe in him as someone truly real, genuine, authentic, not God play-acting at being a man. That's the sort of person those youngsters wanted to believe in. And so do we all at heart. Once we can convince ourselves that at times he was frightened, depressed, angry, hungry, tired, thirsty, puzzled, then we immediately receive a tremendous sense of comfort; the relief that comes when we can say of a friend, 'He knows exactly how I feel because he's been through it all himself.'

A PICTURE OF JESUS

Do we wish in our heart of hearts that photography had been invented 2000 years ago and that Pasolini, the film director, had been a Palestinian contemporary of Jesus? I certainly do, even though I believe his words, 'Blessed are those who have not seen but have believed.' Nevertheless we can turn to the four Gospel writers for a pen portrait

    to Matthew for Jesus the teacher
    to Mark for Jesus the victim
    to Luke for Jesus the Saviour – friend of all
    to John for Jesus the contemporary who lives in our
        world.

These evangelists were not writing a life of Jesus, making a chronicle of sayings and doings in the order in which they happened. They selected, edited, assembled material to meet the different needs of the communities for which they wrote.

CHARACTERISTIC GESTURES

Even though, at first sight, each Gospel writer's impression of Jesus seems to be different, nevertheless there emerges from these four documents a constant picture. It is very well summed up by Canon Rhymes:[2]

Never in the whole course of the Gospel story do we get the impression of one who was putting on an act, adopting a pose, trying to live up to other people's expectations of him. He was at home in the most amazing diversity of surroundings because he was just himself. He played no role, he had one self for one situation, and another self for another situation. He did not see people as 'contacts' to be used; he did not try to possess or to smother people with his emotions; he did not fail to distinguish one person from another and did not lump people into a group; he did not love them for what they might become. He was neither solemn nor superficial; he cared nothing for class distinction or accents; he was not impressed by power and worldly position. He was capable of irony, laughter and tears. He could be angry; shrink naturally from pain ('If it be thy will, take this cup from me'); he could be very outspoken and even, sometimes, contemptuous ('Go and tell that fox [Herod]); he never compromised. In one thing he was utterly consistent; he was always true to the truth he proclaimed for he had made that truth his own in his own living and experience. He lived by the love he proclaimed and that love was, as it always is, both reconciling and divisive. It attracted both love and hostility as love will always attract. It meant just as much the resolute opposition to the evil and destructive in humanity as the encouragement and

[2] *Prayer in the Secular City* by Douglas Rhymes (Lutterworth Press, 1967), pp. 65-6.

seeing what is creative and good in humanity. In one sense he was always an outsider to the world, in another he was the worldly man *par excellence.* He was born and died an outsider: born outside the normal conventions of child-birth – 'no room at the inn', died outside the normal conventions of decent death – on a cross outside the city walls; he never conformed to the world's expectation – he did not stick close to his family, he did not observe his position in society. He lived a rather beatnik sort of life with no settled home, accepting hospitality where he could get it with graciousness and naturalness, in no way feeling under any obligation to those who gave it. He had no hesitation in challenging those in authority. He was very careless of those with whom he associated. He had no worry about his reputation when an ex-tart joined his followers, nor did it worry him that people might think he was homosexual by going round with a group of men and letting John lean on his breast at supper. In all these ways he was an outsider. But yet he was at home with all men: at the age of twelve he could mix naturally in the temple with a group of scholars; he could equally accept the hospitality of Simon the Pharisee, of Zacchaeus the publican; he could promote the gaiety of a wedding by providing extra wine when they had already well drunk; he could share the feelings of Martha and Mary when their brother had died; he could give great gifts of healing to the twisted spirits crying out for integration; he could receive without embarrassment gifts for himself of costly ointment to cleanse his road-dusty feet. He could speak naturally to complete strangers without having to be introduced. He could be at home with fishermen, tax-collectors, tarts, learned men, scribes, religious leaders, Jews and Romans. He could speak with dignity and on equal terms without arrogance to the High Priest and to the Roman Governor; he could afford to ignore with dignity King Herod. He could speak with equal love on the cross to soldiers, to a dying criminal, to those who jeered at him, as to his mother and his best friend: yet that same love could be sufficiently detached to enable him without compunction to leave his home and family.

For discussion

1. Would the members of the group care to say something of the image they have of Jesus Christ? (We must respect the wishes of those who might find the answering of this question too personal.)

2. 'You say that Jesus could not have known about the future if he was a genuine man. Why could he not have used his divine knowledge when he felt the need?' How would you answer this question?

3. 'He grew in wisdom and knowledge' (Luke 2 : 52). Do you think Jesus would have only the primitive scientific ideas of his time, e.g. about creation, the sun, the flat earth, etc.?

4. Do you agree that the idea of a Jesus who 'knew all the answers' makes him seem remote from our human condition?

5. Can you offer any suggestions as to why: (a) so many young people today seem to be less interested (apparently) in organized religion; (b) the seventies will probably be remembered for such productions as *Jesus Christ Superstar* and *Godspell*?

6. This is a comment by Desmond Forrestall[8] which the group may care to discuss: 'Some people have been shocked because *Jesus Christ Superstar* makes Mary

[8] *Superstar or Son of God?* (Veritas Publications, Dublin, 1973).

Magdalen say she has fallen in love with Jesus. But this is the kind of thing that could have happened. In fact, Jesus himself could have fallen in love and married, and raised a family. He remained single because his Father wanted it that way and not because he was some kind of sexless wonder. He remained single because caring for a wife and children would have interfered with the work his Father gave him to do. Many of his followers have done the same thing for the same reason.'

CHAPTER 4

The Image of his Father

'Well, why did Jesus die on the cross?'

'To open the gates of heaven, Father.'

'Come off it, Frank; that's a phrase you learnt and never properly understood, a long time ago. What does it mean?'

'Well, he won heaven for us.'

'That's not much better. Anybody else got a better way of putting it?'

'Well, it's this way. God was angry with men because they had all sinned. So he sent Jesus into the world and said, "You'd better die for that lot. In fact only if you do will I make friends with them again." '

'What do you think the Son felt like at being asked to suffer such a cruel death when he was innocent?'

'I dunno, I suppose he said, "Well I'd better do it if you want me to." '

'Do you think God the Father was pleased when he saw his Son slowly dying in agony on the cross?'

'I can't believe he was.'

'Nor can I.'

GESTURES, EMOTIONS, ACTIONS

As you read through the Gospel, certain phrases descriptive of Jesus seem to occur regularly. In fact, the very regularity of their occurrence helps to build up the image we have of him. For example, one characteristic gesture of his seems to have been a sweeping gaze on those standing around him.

He looked round at them all . . . (Luke 6 : 10)

Jesus looked round . . . and said . . . (Mark 10.23)

And looking round at those sitting in a circle . . . (Mark 3.34)

The emotion most frequently associated with Jesus appears to have been that of pity, compassion.

And when he saw the crowds, his heart was filled with pity for them . . . (Matthew 9.36)

He saw a large crowd and his heart was filled with pity for them . . . (Mark 6.34)

I feel sorry for these people . . . (Mark 8 : 2)

When the Lord saw her his heart was filled with pity for her . . . (Luke 7 : 13)

The activity attributed most frequently to Jesus (apart from his works of healing and preaching) is that of prayer.

While he was praying . . . the Holy Spirit came down upon him. (Luke 3 : 21)

Very early the next morning . . . he went out of town to a lonely place, where he prayed. (Mark 1 : 35)

One time when Jesus was praying alone, the disciples came to him . . . (Luke 9 : 18)

After sending the people away, he went up a hill by himself to pray. (Matthew 14 : 23)

Jesus took Peter, John and James with him and went up a hill to pray. (Luke 9 : 28)

One time Jesus was praying . . . when he finished, one of his disciples said to him, 'Lord teach us to pray . . .' (Luke 11 : 1)

WITH TEARS

Many examples are given in the Gospels of the words Jesus used in his prayers. (See especially Luke 22 : 39-46 and John 17 : 1-26.) His manner of praying is poignantly described in the letter to the Hebrews: 'In his life on

earth, Jesus made his prayers and requests with loud
cries and tears to God, who could save him from death.'
(Hebrews 5:7)

Are we to think that Jesus prayed simply to give us a
good example? 'I'll go out into a desert place where my
apostles will find me so that they will be impressed by
the way I pray. Maybe that will help them to realize
how important prayer is.' Are we to believe that?

Luke describes the agony in the garden: '*In great
anguish* he prayed ever more fervently.' Was this simply
to impress the sleeping disciples? Of course not. Jesus
prayed because he loved his Father. Love for his Father
drove him to pray.

LOVE OF HIS FATHER
This love of his Father is the most striking of all the
characteristics that together go to make up the image of
Jesus painted by all four evangelists. His first (recorded)
words were about his Father, 'Didn't you know that I
had to be in my Father's house?' (Luke 2:49)

His last words on the cross were: 'Father! In your
hands I place my spirit!' (Luke 23:46) On almost every
page of the Gospels we find him speaking about his
Father – he had been sent by the Father, had come to
do what his Father wanted, 'My food is to obey the
will of him who sent me . . .' (John 4:34) There can
be no doubt that this almost obsessive love of his Father
is the driving force of his life.

Whoever does what my Father in heaven wants
him to do is my brother, my sister, my mother.
(Matthew 12:50)

My Father has given me all things. (Matthew 11:
27)

The Father loves his Son and has put everything in
his power. (John 3:35)

... I always do what pleases him. (John 8:29)

The Father and I are one. (John 10:30)

Whoever has seen me has seen the Father. (John 14:9)

(It's almost as though God the Father is pointing to Jesus and saying to me, 'This is the sort of God I am: this is the sort of man I want you to become.')

The living Father sent me, and because of him I live also! (John 6:57)

As the Father sent me, so I send you. (John 20:21) Jesus does not speak of himself as the goal but rather as the way. It is the Father who is the object of both Jesus' existence and ours.

I am the way, the truth, and the life; no one goes to the Father except by me. (John 14:6)

The Hebrew child's familiar name for 'Father' is 'Abba', roughly equivalent to our 'Dad' or 'Daddy'. Jesus too uses this title: 'Abba, all things are possible for you. Take this chalice from me.' It gives us a glimpse of the intimate relationship that existed between Father and Son.

WORKING TO A SCRIPT

Tim Rice, the lyric writer of *Jesus Christ Superstar* has made Judas look around for reasons excusing him from blame. Judas claims that he didn't want to betray Jesus; that he did it almost against his will. Towards the end of the musical, Judas sings:

My mind is darkness now – My God I am sick I've been used

And you knew all the time

God! I'll never ever know why you chose me for your crime

For your foul bloody crime

You have murdered me!

Tim Rice is here placing on Judas' self-pitying lips senti-
ments often expressed about him by schoolchildren:
'Someone had to betray Jesus if God's plan was going
to be carried out. Judas couldn't help it.' It's as though
every detail of the life of Jesus and the actions of the
characters surrounding him were predetermined by the
Father, with Jesus, Mary, Judas, Peter, John, Mary
Magdalen and the others all working to a script.

God's plan! We talk glibly as though we were all
familiar with the Father's design for all men – not 'men'
really, more like puppets on a string – as though we
were looking over his shoulder as he worked on the
blueprints.

A THEORY ONLY

About a thousand years ago, Anselm gave what he believed was the *theory* behind 'God's Plan', and until
recently theologians, both Catholic and Protestant, have
repeated it. It's a relief to know that it is only a theory
and that one does not need to believe it. It can be
summarized as follows:

> Man by his sins offers to a God who is infinitely
> greater than himself an offence that must likewise be
> infinite in its wickedness. But being merely finite and
> capable only of finite actions, man can do nothing of
> himself to repay the infinite debt. That is why God
> sent his Son to become a man – in order to pay off
> this debt. For, since the man Jesus was also truly
> divine, every action of his must have been of infinite
> value in the sight of his Father. But the Father, in
> order to show his hatred for sin, and his love for us
> sinners, demanded his Son go so far as to die on the
> cross.[1]

[1] This neat summary is taken from *For All Men* by J. B.
Walker (Darton, Longman and Todd, 1968), p. 2.

The main disadvantage of this theory is that it makes the Father out to be a monster. His Son preaches that we must forgive our enemies gratuitously – yet the Father was unwilling to do so himself. No wonder we have neglected the Father! He has appeared to have had no part in our salvation.

LOVE NOT JUSTICE

There can be no explanation to the mystery of our redemption. The nearest we can come to the truth is to say that the key to our understanding of it is love not an abstract notion of justice. '. . . God *loved* the world so much that he gave his only Son, so that everyone who believes in him may not die but have eternal life. For God did not send his Son into the world to be its Judge, but to be its Saviour.' (John 3 : 16-17)

It was surely not true that God turned away from men in anger and was persuaded to turn back only by his Son's cruel death. God is not a sadist.[2] It was men who turned away from God. It was men whom Jesus tried to turn back to God by the love he showed through his readiness to accept death. It was not God who was to be reconciled to men : 'It was God who reconciled us to himself through Christ . . .' (2 Corinthians 5 : 18 – Jerusalem Bible translation)

THE FACTS

Let's look briefly again at the events that led proud and 'blind' and cruel men to bring about the death of Jesus. For, let's be clear on this, it was men who put Jesus to

---

[2] These implications would not have been either understood or intended by St Anselm. But a misreading of his theory could and has certainly produced in young people this sort of reaction. For example, a frequent question asked is, 'What did Jesus think about his Father demanding that he should die such a horrible death?'

death, not God.

Jesus came to tell men the Good News that God is a Father to all.

That if men wish to live in God's way they must treat each other as brothers.

That they must serve, share with, care for and forgive even their enemies.

The leaders of his time would not accept this teaching.

He could have kept quiet.

He could have run away. He could have left the country quite easily even to the moment of his arrest.

In fact, it is quite clear from his agony in the garden that he was tempted to quit.

But loving his Father, remaining true to his Father's message for men, loving men and wanting to convince men of God's unfailing love for them he underwent the terror of suffering and death.

'He was humble and walked the path of obedience to death – his death on the cross. For this reason God raised him to the highest place above, and gave him the name that is greater than any other name.' (Philippians 2:8-9)

'God raised him' says St Paul. So also Peter: 'You killed him . . . but God raised him.' (Acts 2:23-4) 'God raised this very Jesus from the dead. (Acts 2:32) 'You killed the prince of life. God, however, raised him from the dead. (Acts 3:15)

THE FATHER'S REWARD

It's as though the Father is saying, 'I want men to know that I love them and want them to be with me. I sent my Son to be man, to tell his fellow men the Good News of my love, even though I knew that men would kill him. He stayed true to my word, so I have raised him to my right hand.'

Jesus saved us not only through his death on the cross. He saved us in his rising from the tomb. He rose to a new life. It was much more than the revivification of a corpse. Lazarus came back to life again but, one day, he died. Jesus came back to life in a much more wonderful way. He would never die again.

By our baptism, then, we were buried with him and shared his death, in order that, just as Christ was raised from death by the glorious power of the Father, so also we might live a new life . . . For we know that Christ has been raised from death and will never die again – death has no more power over him. The death he died was death to sin, once and for all, and the life he now lives is life to God. In the same way you are to think of yourselves as dead to sin but alive to God in union with Christ Jesus. (Romans 6:4-11)

For discussion

1. Have the members of the group any comments to make about (a) the prayer of Jesus to his Father, (b) the love of Jesus for his Father?

2. Jesus called his Father 'Abba'. Do you think we too should be able to speak in such an intimate way to God?

3. Have you any comments to make on the freedom of Judas not to betray Jesus, on the possibility that Peter need not have denied Jesus, on the temptation of Jesus to 'want this cup of poison to pass away'.

4. Do you agree that 'the key to our understanding of our redemption is love, not justice'?

Concluding Prayer
Lord Jesus Christ, you are a man like us

blood of our blood,
and, bearing the name of God,
you are exalted in his light.
the Son of God.
But do not be remote from us,
hidden and unapproachable.
Pray for us with your human voice
and send us your Spirit
that we may come to life
and make this world
a fit place to live in
and meet him, your Father and ours,
now and in the life to come.[3]

[3] From *Your Word Is Near* by Huub Oosterhuis (Newman Press, 1968), p. 97.

CHAPTER 5

Jesus Now: Jesus Here

'Ladies and Gentlemen, you will soon be alighting from
the coach at the top of the Mount of Olives. It was from
this summit just east of Jerusalem that Jesus began his
Palm Sunday procession. If you look out of the right-
hand windows you will see the route he took into Jerusalem.

'It was also from the Mount of Olives that Jesus said
goodbye to his apostles and ascended into heaven.

'I am going to ask Father Smith to read the appro-
priate passage from the Acts of the Apostles.'

'The reading, my dear brethren, is from Chapter 1,
verses 6-12. "When the Apostles met together with
Jesus they asked him, 'Lord, will you at this time give
the Kingdom back to Israel?' Jesus said to them, 'The
times and occasions are set by my Father's own authority, and it is not for you to know when they will be.
But you will be filled with power when the Holy Spirit
comes on you, and you will be witnesses for me in
Jerusalem, in all of Judea and Samaria, and to the ends
of the earth.' After saying this, he was taken up into
heaven as they watched him; and a cloud hid him
from their sight." This is the end of the reading.'

'Thank you, Father. Just before you walk to the site
of the Ascension, I have two things to tell you: the
first is that outside the church you will see a man with
a camel who will offer you an opportunity of sitting on

*the camel's back while you have your photograph taken.
The second thing is that when you enter the grounds of
the garden, you will see a rock on which are imbedded
the footprints of our Saviour just before he ascended.*

*'You may leave the coach now. Please be back in half
an hour when we leave for our hotel in Bethany.'*

What does the Christian make of the Ascension?
Would he believe in or would he smile at the 'footprints
in the rock'? Every year this feast day comes round.
What is it we celebrate? If Jesus rose up slowly and
majestically before the apostles' eyes, what happened
to him after a cloud hid him from their sight? Did he
disappear? Or did he continue to ascend and, if so, for
how long? Was it somewhere in outer space that his
journey ended? Did his risen body, which had appeared
and disappeared, entered rooms despite locked doors,
need to make any journey to heaven? For that matter,
can we say that heaven is located in a particular place,
or that it occupies space?

These questions are not asked facetiously. We really
need to face up to the meaning of the mysteries we
profess our belief in. It's simply not enough to recite
Sunday after Sunday, 'He ascended into heaven – sitteth
at the right hand of God the Father almighty.' These
phrases must mean something to us. One recalls that
the 'penny' catechism said we do not need to believe
that Jesus literally sits at the right hand of God. May
we expect to be allowed the same liberal interpretation
of the Ascension?

WHERE WAS JESUS?
When Jesus was not appearing to his friends after his
Resurrection, where was he? Let's put the question
more precisely by looking at a particular time on Easter

day: between the appearance to the disciples on the road to Emmaus and the appearance in the upper room to the apostles, where was he? Or to put it another way: the various appearances related in the Gospels would amount to no more than a few hours' duration at most; if there were a literal 40 days between Resurrection and Ascension, how did Jesus occupy the rest of his time? Where was he? What was he doing?

The answer must surely be that he was already by his Resurrection *with the Father*. And it was from the Father that he made himself visible and tangible from time to time to his believing friends.

Let us consider his meeting with Mary Magdalen on the morning of Easter. Jesus tells her not to cling to him. Things are no longer as they were before. The ordinary intimacy of earth is over. Jesus' place is now with the Father. He speaks of his ascension. 'I have not yet ascended. Go to my brethren and say to them, I am ascending to my Father and your Father, to my God and your God.' (John 20:17)

These words leave room for various explanations, but their central message is clear. 'Resurrection implies being with the Father . . .' If that is so, what are we to make of Luke's account of the Ascension?

The message of the Gospel is not that Jesus, after being hidden by the cloud, went on up through the atmosphere till he finally came to the Father. Christ's glorified humanity does not pass through distances as we do. And then the Father, or heaven, is not 'above'. The notion of 'above' was chosen because the vault of heaven with its light, its spaciousness, and its freedom, is a splendid symbol of the place of God. But the Father to whom Jesus went is not bound to any place.[1]

[1] *A New Catechism* (Search Press, 1970), p. 190.

UNSEEN PRESENCE

We will remain nearer the truth if we do not associate ideas of bodily movement with the Ascension. The Ascension was rather the last of many appearances of Jesus to his friends. It was a symbolic gesture indicating the final triumph of his work as man. From now on he would no longer be visible, but he would still be present in our world.

A cloud symbolized the presence of God to the Jews. 'A cloud hid him from their sight' indicates the fulfilment of Jesus' promise of his continued presence. 'I will be with you,' he had just said, 'always, to the end of the age.' (Matthew 28:20)

Jesus did not leave the earth at his Ascension. He is present and we can meet him today and every day. We meet him in each other: ' "When did we ever see you sick or in prison, and visit you?" The King will answer back, "I tell you, indeed, whenever you did this for one of the least important of these brothers of mine, you did it for me." ' (Matthew 25:39-40)

We meet him when we are gathered together in his name. Do we really believe him when he says, 'Where two or three come together in my name, I am there with them' (Matthew 18:20)? He is present and we hear his voice when the Scriptures are read in the church.[2] By his Spirit, he lives on in his Church and in the sacraments of the Church. We need not envy the Palestinian friends of Jesus. We are as close to him today as were Peter, James and John. The most special occasions on which we meet him in the various situations of our journey to the Father, we call the sacraments.

[2] See par. 7 of Vatican II's Decree on the Liturgy.

MEETINGS WHICH CHANGE US

Every time we celebrate any of the sacraments, we are meeting Jesus today in our lives. People who met him in Palestine, if they had faith and trust in him, had their lives completely transformed. If they had no trust in him, he could do nothing for them. In Nazareth, Matthew tells us, 'He did not perform many miracles . . . because they did not have faith.' (Matthew 13:58) It was not so much that Jesus worked miraculous cures on people in order to get them to believe in him. He first seemed to demand faith in himself, and if that was present, help was forthcoming. 'Go, *your faith* has saved you,' he said on more than one occasion after a miracle of healing.

. . . a certain blind man was sitting by the road, begging. When he heard the crowd passing by he asked, 'What is this?' 'Jesus of Nazareth is passing by,' they told him. He cried out, 'Jesus! Son of David! Have mercy on me!' The people in front scolded him and told him to be quiet. But he shouted even more loudly, 'Son of David! Have mercy on me!' So Jesus stopped and ordered that the blind man be brought to him. . . . 'What do you want me to do for you?' 'Sir,' he answered, 'I want to see again.' Then Jesus said to him, 'See! Your faith has made you well.' At once he was able to see, and he followed Jesus, giving thanks to God. (Luke 18:35-43)

If the blind man's faith had not led him to shout for help and disregard the scolding crowds, Jesus' presence nearby would not automatically have cured him. It was his faith in Jesus that brought about a total transformation in his life.

It is the same with our meetings today with him. When we meet him in the Sacrament of Penance or in the Holy Eucharist, we must really want to be changed and believe that he can transform us. These meetings with him will result in our becoming more mature, more human, more free, more happy, to the extent that we have faith in him.

ALL THIS AND HEAVEN TOO

It's not just a case of meeting him in order to make my entry into heaven more sure. It's a case of meetings with Jesus making me more able to serve the world. That's our job as Christians, after all. We must allow Jesus to continue through us the work he first began in Palestine.

Any work that dispels ignorance and disorder
gets rid of blindness and prejudice
relieves suffering and pain
builds up and restores hope
brings people together in harmony and peace
is the work of Jesus through his Spirit in the world. We must work with him, empowered by his Spirit, in making the world which God so loved, our world, a better place, so that at the end the Son may hand it over fully perfected to the Father from whom it came.

Father God, your glory it is
that our concern should be
to live happily as men.
May we see at last
this world, cured, restored,
your name hallowed among us,
peace on earth
and may we see this come about
for the sake of him
who lives with you,
Jesus, our Lord.
We ask you, Father,
to let us see this man,

knowing that who sees him
beholds you, the Father,
and this is enough
for us as for this world
and for all times. Amen.[8]

For discussion

1. What has the group's understanding of the Ascension been? What significance has it held for you individually?

2. We speak about the 'real' presence of Jesus in the Holy Eucharist. Does this mean that his other presences are unreal?

3. Do the sacraments affect you if you have no faith in Jesus? If our meetings with Jesus are to change us, what is necessary on our part?

4. Have you thought of the sacraments as meetings with Jesus today? And have you thought of those meetings as able to make you 'more mature, more human, more free, more happy'?

5. How do we collaborate with Jesus in 'making this world a better place'?

[8] *Your Word Is Near* by Huub Oosterhuis.

CHAPTER 6

Our Parish Mass – a Celebration

Agnes noticed Joe's cough for the first time in November. 'You ought to see the doctor about it,' she told him. 'You don't usually cough even when you have a cold.'

'It's those cigarettes, Dad,' said Clair, the youngest of their four children. 'You know what the adverts say – "The best tip of all, give 'em up." '

Joe eventually went to the doctor. And from the doctor to the hospital for an X-ray. A week passed by before he received a note to say he should visit the surgery, and soon.

'It's not good news,' said Dr Thomas. 'They've spotted something which requires surgery. I want you to be in hospital by tonight.'

'Tonight? But that's impossible. I can't just drop everything. It will be at least a week before . . .'

The doctor cut him short. 'I think you ought to know that your operation is regarded as an emergency. Each day's delay is going to make the operation more serious.'

'Is it lung cancer, doctor?' he asked. Dr Thomas hesitated. 'There is the beginning of a growth,' he said. 'They may well have to remove a lung.'

Joe was operated on three days later. For a while his condition was critical. Even Agnes doubted his ability to get better, and she prepared herself for the worst. Every night she and the children prayed for him together. They knelt round 'his chair' as they prayed and wished with all their heart that he was back with them again.

Sixteen days after the operation he began to regain his colour. He could smile and began to enjoy a short conversation. Four weeks later and the surgeon was able to tell him that as far as one could see it was possible to give him a completely clean bill of health.

Three days later Joe was back at home. Agnes and the children gave him a week to recover his old self, then they told him what they were going to do. 'A party,' they said. 'We're going to have a thanksgiving-glad-to-have-you-back-with-us-party. We've invited the grandparents, several of the uncles and aunts, three of your friends from work. Oh no, it won't be anything elaborate. Just an ordinary meal, and a bottle of wine.'

'It's a bit like the party for the prodigal son,' said Clair, 'except it's for the prodigal father. You were lost and now you are found' – she mimicked Fr Johnson's pulpit manner – 'You were dead (or nearly so) and now you are alive again. So let's have a celebration.'

On the Sunday following the party (which incidentally was a great success), Joe and Agnes were at Mass with their family. It was by a strange coincidence that Fr Johnson decided to speak about the Mass as a celebration. 'We speak of the Mass as a celebration, but what, in fact, is a celebration?' he asked the congregation, not really expecting anyone to reply. 'I looked it up in the dictionary last night,' he continued, 'and this is what it said: "A celebration is an act of observing and commemorating, by social ceremonies, an occasion or event which gives rise to feelings of joy and thankfulness."

'And what is this event that "gives rise to feelings of joy and thankfulness" which we celebrate at Mass? It's not the death of Jesus, is it? We proclaim his death but we don't celebrate it. You can't be happy at a death. Now what it is we celebrate is that Jesus didn't stay dead. He rose to a new life.

'This is the happy ending. Or rather this is the happy beginning – the beginning of a new life. Because his life didn't end in the grave. Oh yes, his friends thought for a time that he was a goner,' (Fr Johnson's parishioners didn't object to his colloquial language), 'but then he came back to them again, visible and tangible. I think the biggest understatement of all time is in St John's Gospel where the evangelist describes the first sight the apostles had of their friend, their risen Lord. This is what John writes: "The disciples were filled with joy when they saw the Lord." Pretty weak language for a group of lads who must have felt like jumping for joy.

'I don't suppose many of you have had the experience of someone very close to you being in a critical state, hovering between life and death for days,' (this is where Joe and Agnes exchanged glances) 'but if you have,' the priest continued, 'you'll know how the apostles felt when Jesus came back to them. Of course, he had been really dead and not just sick. And this is what made it all so wonderful.

'But the heart of the matter is that we are in the same position as the apostles. It's the same Jesus. He's not gone away. He didn't go away on Ascension day. He said "I'll stay with you always even to the end of the world." He's in our world now. And at Mass we celebrate this fact. We celebrate the fact that he passed through suffering and death and came out triumphantly living.

'The fact that he passed through death and rose again is good news for us. It makes sense of our lives. If he hadn't risen, we'd have had it. We'd be just like our pets – our dogs and cats and budgies – after a brief life, extinction, nothingness. Whereas we know that because of Jesus' conquering death we will conquer death too. Isn't this something to celebrate?'

A two-year-old at the back of the church raised his voice. 'Ga-ga-ga,' he said, much to the embarrassment of his mother on whose knee he writhed.

'You see,' continued Fr Johnson with a smile, 'even that little one agrees with me. We say "Christ *has* died, Christ *is* risen," (note the present tense) "Christ *will* come again." And this is great good news for us. That's why we celebrate.

'Now one of the things about a celebration is that you can't do it alone. You must be with other people – with friends. Usually at a celebration we eat and drink. It would be hard to think of a celebration without food and drink.' (The children looked at Agnes, their mother, who had spent so long getting the meal for their celebration ready.) 'This is how it should be at Mass. We should be friends together. It should be a happy occasion.

'I don't blame you,' continued the priest, 'but sometimes I get the feeling that you don't think of the Mass as a happy happening. You don't seem to want to sing. Some of you look terribly sad. It could be my fault. But you know what I should like it to be – a get-together of friends which we should be glad to take part in, a celebration in which we praise and thank God our Father for raising his Son Jesus to life again; in which we are glad to meet Jesus alive and with us now, who, if we trust him, can transform our lives, can make us more truly human by the power of his Spirit. It was one of the Vatican documents, I think, that said, "He who follows Christ the perfect man will himself become more fully human."

'However, I've said enough. Let's now stand and respond together to God's word by saying together the "I believe".'

For discussion

1. What is your opinion as to the various reasons why people go to Mass on Sunday? Divide your congregation into
     (a) children
     (b) teenagers
     (c) newly-weds
     (d) the elderly
   and give a separate assessment for each group.
2. Do you think that teenagers and newly-weds have the same attitude to the obligation of Sunday Mass as older people have?
3. Does the Mass appear to you to be a celebration? Do most people at Mass seem to enjoy it? Should they?
4. What do you think the phrase means: 'He who follows Christ the perfect man becomes himself more fully human'?
5. Who can do what to make the Mass more of a celebration, a happy happening?

CHAPTER 7

God Speaks to Us

Jack: I think they've just put it in to spin the Mass out a bit.

Sam: Put what in?

Jack: All that stuff that's read out at the beginning of Mass. I can see the point of reading the Gospel. It's only right that we should know what our Lord said; but all that stuff about the Jews living years and years before Christ – I honestly can't see what that's got to do with us. After all, we're not Jews, are we? I expect they are reading that sort of thing out in the synagogue in Mather Avenue every Saturday morning.

Sam: Well, I suppose there must be a reason for it else the Church wouldn't do it.

Mary: Not long ago we had a meeting of the Young Wives' Club and we had a talk from a priest from the seminary. It was all about the Bible, or was it the Old Testament? I forget now.

Sam: But the Bible is the Old Testament.

Jack: No it's not. The Bible is the Old Testament and the New Testament – both together go to make the Bible.

Mary: Anyway this priest said that the Old Testament was probably the only thing Jesus read. He said that the whole Bible was the inspired word of God, not just the New Testament.

Jack: Whether it's inspired or not, it doesn't make it any easier to understand. The very name puts me off – 'Old Testament'! A thing can only sell today if

it's new. Who wants anything old? It sounds sort of
second hand, second best.

And then that word 'Testament'. It reminds me of
'last will and Testament'.

Mary: Well it is really a bit like that. It means 'an
agreement'. 'Old' means 'first'. So Old Testament
means 'The First Agreement', or 'Pact', that God
made with his people. In the books of the Old Testament you can read about the way people responded
to God's agreement. Some were generous with God
but many were mean. At least that's what this priest
said.

Sam: I've got to hand it to you, Mary – you are a good
listener! What you are saying then is that the New
Testament must be the New Agreement God made
with men when he sent his Son into our world.

Mary: Yes, that's right. You see you can only understand a lot of the New Testament if you understand
a bit about the Old. The priest at the Young Wives'
Club had a copy of the *Jerusalem Bible* with him and
he showed us an example. It's in the first chapter of
St Luke's Gospel in that part where Mary is being
asked to be the mother of our Lord. The priest
showed us the margin of just this small section and
it gives about a dozen references to the Old Testament. You can make good sense of what Mary said
only if you know about those references. It also goes
to show how familiar Mary was with the Old Testament. If it was important for her, it should be important for us.

Sam: Let's just come back to Sunday Mass again. About
ten minutes or so is spent while we listen to the
readings. The way it is with me is that quite often I
can't hear the reader, or he doesn't pronounce the
words right. The other day he kept on saying 'forni-

cation' when he should have been saying 'fortifica-
tion'. Another time, he said, 'We will all put on im-
morality', when he meant 'immortality'. It just shows
what sort of sense it made to him. Then another thing
– the readings are all about different things. I've got
the little sheet of paper with me that gives today's
Mass.

Jack: You should have left that in church for the next
Mass.

Sam: I'll give it to the boy to bring to the evening
Mass. I just wanted to have another look to see if I
could make sense of it, but I can't.

Mary: Well here's Syd. He read it out this morning.
He ought to know what it means.

Jack: Yes, Syd, come and join us and try and throw a
bit of light in our direction.

Syd: I don't know whether I'll be able to do that.
Fr Johnson just helps me to practise the reading.
He doesn't tell me a great deal about the meaning of
it.

Sam: Well today's first reading was from a book called
'Numbers'. Numbers of what? Did the Jews play
bingo?

Syd: No, I know that much anyway. The book is called
'Numbers' because it begins with a census of the
population – in other words numbers of people.

Sam: Fair enough, Syd. Let's just move on to the first
sentence: 'The Lord came down in the cloud.' How
did he come down? Was it God the Father, or God
the Son or the Holy Spirit?

Syd: Well it can't have been God the Son or the Holy
Spirit because the Jews didn't exactly know that there
were three Persons in God till Jesus told them. For
the Jews living before Christ, God was really one
Person although there are hints now and again that

they didn't think of this one Person as being all alone.
As to how God came down, I don't know. What
they saw I don't know.

Sam: Even so the rest of the reading is just double-
dutch to me. And then we've got this – what do you
call it – 'responsal psalm'. What a mouthful!

Syd: Well that's like a hymn and it's supposed to help
you reflect on what's gone before. The psalms were
like the folk songs we sing today.

Mary: But just a minute Syd, can you tell us how the
whole lot hang together?

Syd: I can tell only as much as I know and that's not
very much. I think it's this way: for the reading at
Mass the whole of the Bible is spread over three
years, although parts are the same for every year –
Advent, Lent, Easter-time, for example. Think of the
Gospels first, Matthew's Gospel is Year 1, Mark's
Gospel is Year 2, and Luke's Gospel is Year 3.

Jack: And where do we get St John's Gospel?

Syd: That comes in round about Easter.

Sam: Well according to this we're on Year 2 because
the Gospel is Mark's.

Syd: Correct. The way it is is this: the people in the
Vatican who fixed these readings first chose the particular section of Mark's Gospel for today. Then they
looked through the Old Testament for a bit that
would match up with it, throw light on it – a sort of
twin piece which would come first. This Old Testament bit is then followed by the psalm – the folk
song – then the Gospel.

Sam: But wait a moment. There's something else here.
Between the Old Testament part and the New Testament Gospel part there's a bit from a letter written
by St James. How does that fit in?

Syd: It doesn't fit in really. If you have a good memory

you would realize that we've been having chunks of that letter for the last four weeks. In other words the Old Testament bit, the psalm, and the Gospel all go together. The bit of the letter (and it's most often one of Paul's letters) is just thrown in – and it may or may not have anything to do with the other readings.

I suppose a clever preacher might be able to blend the whole lot together and say, 'This is the message that God gives you today.'

For discussion

1. What is your honest reaction to the readings at Mass? Do you wish you could understand them better or would you be as happy without them?
2. Do you think that the Bible is a very special book?
3. Can you recall any parts of the Bible that have helped you?
4. What about your parish? Are there lay readers? Can you hear them? Are they volunteers or were they asked? Should they understand what the reading is about before they read it? Should they be trained? How?

CHAPTER 8

Good News for Now

They were good parishioners who had given up a Sunday to have a 'Day of Recollection'. At the end of the day the group of them met before tea to talk over various points: the Mass, difficult children, family prayers. Finally, we talked about the readings at Mass and how difficult some of them were to understand. I had expected them to say that the Old Testament was the main cause of confusion. But the group was equally critical of the New Testament; and not only of the Epistles (understandably), but also of the Gospels. One man said, 'The Gospels really are very old fashioned.'

'What do you mean?' I asked.

'Well, they're all about things that don't concern us any more – sheep and shepherds, water, fishing, sowing seed. And some of the stories are a bit silly – who'd go down the M.6 sowing seed?' (This was a reference to the parable of the sower – 'Some seed fell on the roadway.') 'And there'd be union trouble if employees got paid the way one parable makes out they should be.'

Someone else said: 'We had a caller the other night at our house who gave us a Gospel by St Mark. I tried to read it but by about Chapter 4 I gave it up. In any case, I wasn't so sure I wanted to read it. My cousin told me that she once found her husband reading the Gospels. He was on sick leave. She had a premonition that something was going to happen to him.'

'Well, did anything?' I asked.

'Yes, he died soon after of a cerebral thrombosis.'

Someone else said, 'Why can't we just have the prayer before and after the consecration, and then Communion? These readings really are a waste of time.'

The only way for people to overcome this antipathy towards the New Testament is to realize that it really is God our Father speaking to us today about our lives now. It is not just a book about the past. Nor are the Gospels simply four lives of Jesus, four biographies, which might be summarized into a contemporary non-religious *Who's Who* in a manner such as this:

Jesus Christ: More correctly, Jesus *the* Christ. ('Christ' is a title, not a surname.) Born of poor parents, around the year 4 BC in bustling Bethlehem, 70 miles away from his home hamlet of Nazareth. In a stable. Reputed son of Joseph, an odd-job man in Nazareth (pop. 950) and Miriam (Mary), both parents descended from line of King David. For some 30 years, he showed no exceptional talent, but helped his parents in the family business. At about the age of 30, left home. Asked his second cousin, a prophet, John, to baptize him, then began to gather together twelve special friends, whom he instructed in his way of living and thinking. Apparently possessed a magnetic personality since these friends left everything to follow him. Most of them later died for his cause. He attracted large numbers of followers who said he 'spoke with authority'. He also had remarkable powers of healing.

At first his preaching resulted in success and popularity, but later it became obvious that the religious leaders of his time did not share the people's enthusiasm. His main message was that God (whom he claimed to be his Father in a unique way) was also a real Father to all, that he was a Father who would never forsake men whatever they might do; that men must be like their Father in that they must love and forgive friend and foe alike, that people will be finally judged mainly according to the way they have treated others. 'As long as you did it to one of those, the least of my brethren,' he said, 'you did it to me.'

Two overriding characteristics appear to have been, first, his almost obsessive love of his Father ('I always do what pleases my Father. My food is to do the will of him who sent me') and, second, his compassion for ordinary people, especially the defenceless, the handicapped, the down-trodden. These two characteristics finally brought about his death. Although free to escape, because of his desire to remain true to the Person he called 'Father' and to convince men that his Father loved all men, he endured a shameful death. One of his friends, Judas, betrayed him. Another, Peter, denied knowing him. All the others except one deserted him. On the orders of Pontius Pilate, governor of Judea (later exiled) he was crucified on Friday, 3 April 29 AD, and died at 3.00 p.m. on that day. On the Sunday following, a number of people claimed that they had seen him alive again — and that he promised never to leave this world ('I will be with you always even to the end of the world'). His followers today are called Christians and they believe that Jesus is still alive and even now able to transform the lives of those who believe in him.

That is a 'life of Christ' as it might be summarized by a non-believer. Notice how it appears to have been written with no special audience in mind. In contrast to this, the Gospels were written by believers and each of them wrote for a particular readership.

FOUR PORTRAITS

The *Gospel of Matthew* appears to have been written especially for convert Jews, because the author constantly refers to the Old Testament. He presumes that his readers are familiar with it. He is interested in presenting Jesus THE SUPREME TEACHER, far greater than the teacher, Moses.

The *Gospel of Mark* is most probably based upon the stories about Jesus which Peter preached to the Christian converts of Rome. Mark's style of writing is quite different from Matthew's, more vivid through giving more detail. [Compare, for example, the way Matthew relates the storm at sea (Matthew 8:23-7) with the way Mark writes about the same incident (Mark 4:35-41).] Mark's is the shortest Gospel – one can read it in less than an hour. Almost one quarter of it is devoted to the Passion and death of Jesus, perhaps because the people for whom he wrote were suffering persecution. Mark seems concerned not just with Jesus the MAN, but with Jesus the VICTIM SON OF GOD.

The *Gospel of Dr Luke* is homely, and contains many human touches. We are indebted to Luke for stories and incidents portraying forgiveness. Luke is concerned to show how the Good News (the meaning of 'Gospel') spread from humble Nazareth to the capital city, Jerusalem. (In the second half of his Gospel, called 'The Acts of the Apostles', Luke shows how the same Good News travelled to far-off and sophisticated Rome.) In Luke, Jesus is most of all portrayed as SAVIOUR AND FRIEND. Luke is the only Gentile amongst all the authors of the Bible books and he wrote his Gospel for fellow Gentiles.

The *Gospel of John*, probably written some sixty years or so after the Resurrection, is concerned most of all to show that Jesus is ALIVE WITH US NOW. 'Happy are those who have *not* seen and believed,' Jesus says in this Gospel. (Whereas in Matthew, Jesus says, 'Happy the eyes that see what you see.') The actions ascribed to Jesus are followed by an explanation – usually in the form of a sermon. Whereas the Gospel of Mark (and to some extent those of Matthew and Luke) concentrate very much on the historical man Jesus, John wants his disciples to see that Jesus is more than a historical figure, he is the 'Word of God made flesh' and very much living with us now.

LAPSE OF TIME

One must remember that the lapse of time between the Resurrection and the publication of the first Gospel was about thirty-five years (the space of time between the start of World War II and 1974). It is natural that the intervening events should have affected the four writers' *choice and presentation* of material about Jesus. A person writing a life of Winston Churchill in the 1970s would write a very different biography from the one he would have written 30 years earlier. In the same way, the four Gospel writers (evangelists), in writing about Jesus many years afterwards, were very much influenced by what had happened in the intervening time. They were concerned, for example, to apply Jesus' words to the situation of their time and to the difficulties which contemporary Christians had to face. On a few occasions, one saying of Jesus is applied by one evangelist to one situation, by another to a situation that is quite different.

NOT A DIARY

One must keep in mind that the four Gospels are not four diaries of day-to-day events in the life of Jesus. Far from it. This wasn't the writers' concern. Their aim was to edit, select, even on occasions adapt, his sayings and his actions to the needs of the Christian communities for whom they were writing. One of the remarkable things about the Gospels is that no matter how often one reads them, one always discovers something new. Fr Alec Jones, the editor of a contemporary translation, told me: 'Although I've read the Gospels five or six thousand times (!), at each new reading I discover something I've never noticed before.' Try this for yourself now. The following four passages are chosen as demonstrating the different interests and techniques of the four Gospel writers.

For discussion

1. From *Matthew*, read slowly Chapter 7 (the conclusion of the Sermon on the Mount). After reading, try to answer these questions:

   Why are we not to judge others?

   What humorous comparison does Jesus suggest in this matter of judging others?

   What is meant by 'throwing pearls in front of pigs'?

   'Ask and you will receive' – why are not all prayers answered?

   What is 'the narrow gate'?

   How are we to recognize whether 'prophets' are true or false?

2. From *Mark*, read Chapter 10:17-30.

   What was the question the young man asked?

   What was the meaning of Jesus' reply?

   Was the young man satisfied with this reply?

   How did he react to Jesus' advice?

   Oxen and asses were more common in Palestine. Why then did Jesus use the 'way-out' example of 'camel'?

Why is it hard for rich men to live in God's way?

What had Peter given up to follow Jesus?

What is the meaning of the reward Jesus offers to those who follow him?

3. From *Luke*, read Chapter 15:11-31.

How would you describe the behaviour of the younger son?

Does it appear to embitter the father?

How does the son lose his money?

Does love of his father drive the son back home?

What hint in the story implies that the father was hoping for the son's return?

What word would describe the character-defect of the older brother?

What right has the older brother to accuse the younger of going with prostitutes?

What message or messages does this story convey to you – about God, forgiveness, sin, yourself?

4. From *John*, read Chapter 15:1-17.

What does 'bear fruit' mean?

How do we 'remain in Jesus'?

What conditions does Jesus lay down if our prayers are to be answered?

What is to be the extent of our love for one another?

Why does Jesus call us his friends?

Postscript

There are many good translations of the New Testament. Here are the titles of two:

Good News for Modern Man (Fontana)

The Jerusalem New Testament (Hodder and Stoughton). An excellent simplified New Testament is *New World* by Alan Dale (Oxford University Press). *Companion to the Good News* (Fontana) presents easy introductions to each of the books of the New Testament.

The Bible Reading Fellowship offers a remarkable range of helpful literature. Especially useful are their notes for daily Bible reading. The address is: St Michael's House, 2 Elizabeth Street, London, SW1.

CHAPTER 9

The Case of the Hasty Letter Writer

This is how St Paul described the sort of life he lived:
'I have worked much harder, I have been in prison more times, I have been whipped much more, and I have been near death more often. Five times I was given the thirty-nine lashes by the Jews; three times I was whipped by the Romans, and once I was stoned; I have been in three shipwrecks, and once I spent twenty-four hours in the water. In my many travels I have been in danger from floods and from robbers, in danger from fellow Jews and from Gentiles; there have been dangers in the cities, dangers in the wilds, dangers on the high seas, and dangers from false friends. There has been work and toil; often I have gone without sleep; I have been hungry and thirsty; I have often been without enough food, shelter, or clothing. And, not to mention other things, every day I am under the pressure of my concern for all the churches.' (2 Corinthians 11:23-8)

At Sunday morning Mass, the second reading is most often taken from one of Paul's letters to Christian converts at Rome, or Corinth, or one of the other communities he had founded throughout his hectic life. All we hear at Mass are snippets of a letter. Small wonder that they make little sense to so many people. To appreciate the meaning of such short extracts we should really hear the whole letter, or at least know what it is all about. We should know something of the pressing problems that provoked the letter to the local church.

Paul didn't say to himself, 'Who shall I write to now?' He wrote only because the circumstances of the people to whom he addressed himself demanded that he write. Before we examine the sort of problems that provoked the letters let's take a look at Paul's background.

THREE CULTURES

When Jesus was about fifteen years old, Saul (later to be called Paul) was born. His home town was Tarsus, a city situated on the eastern Mediterranean coast of present-day Turkey, some five hundred miles northwards from Nazareth. Today Tarsus is little more than a collection of hovels. Then, it was a magnificent city boasting its own university. Paul's parents were prosperous citizens and strict Jews. Paul himself was a mixture of three cultures: part Roman, he was later to appeal for justice on the grounds of his Roman citizenship; part Greek, in that this was his everyday language; Jewish by birth, and very proud of it. This cosmopolitan background was to stand him in good stead in his missionary work.

TENT-MAKER BY TRADE

He went to Jerusalem to a Jewish 'seminary'. A man named Gamaliel was his professor. (See Acts 5:34.) After a few years he returned to Tarsus to help his father in the tent-making family firm. But Paul's zeal was greater than anything Tarsus could demand of him. Before long he was back in Jerusalem. We first meet him in the New Testament at Stephen's execution. The executioners took off their cloaks and left them 'in charge of a young man named Saul' (Acts 7:58). 'And Saul approved of his murder.'

THE FANATIC

His zeal for the purity of the Jewish religion led him to offer his services to persecute those who believed that Jesus was the Messiah who, having been put to death, was now believed by his followers to be still alive. 'In the meantime Saul kept up his violent threats of murder against the disciples of the Lord. He went to the High Priest and asked for letters of introduction to the Jewish synagogues in Damascus, so that if he should find any followers of the Way of the Lord there, he would be able to arrest them, both men and women, and take them back to Jerusalem.' (Acts 9:1-2)

PAUL MEETS JESUS

'On his way to Damascus, as he came near the city, suddenly a light from the sky flashed round him. He fell to the ground and heard a voice saying to him, "Saul, Saul! Why do you persecute me?" "Who are you, Lord?" he asked. "I am Jesus whom you persecute," the voice said.' (Acts 9:3-5.) This meeting with Jesus is described by Paul five times. Obviously it is the turning-point of Paul's life. But it is more than that. The words of Jesus identifying himself with the Christians whom Paul persecutes is the foundation of the doctrine which he is going to preach for the rest of his life: Jesus is to be found in everyone we meet, and we are in Jesus.

ACCEPTED BY THE APOSTLES

After a long 'retreat' in the desert, Paul went to Jerusalem to introduce himself to the apostles. To the orthodox Jews there, Paul was a renegade. It was inevitable that his presence should stir up trouble. The apostles therefore took him to Caesarea and put him on the boat back to Tarsus. There he might have remained if he hadn't been invited to look after the increasing number of Gentile converts. For we must remember that at first the apostles thought of the Way Jesus had founded as open only to Jews. It took some time before they were convinced that anyone, Jew or Gentile, could be a follower of Jesus Christ. When increasing numbers of Gentiles asked for baptism, the apostles were uncertain how to cope with the situation and sent Barnabas to find Paul. 'Then Barnabas went to Tarsus to look for Saul. When he found him, he brought him to Antioch. For a whole year the two met with the people of the church and taught a large group.' (Acts 11:25-6) At the end of the year, Paul set out on his first missionary journey. He was to travel some thirty thousand miles on foot and more than ten thousand miles by boat. He spent 22 years of his life travelling, often sleeping rough. In the country he was in continual danger from bandits. In the towns his life was constantly in peril from Jewish religious leaders who regarded him as a turncoat.

A GREAT DICTATOR

As far as we know, all Paul's letters were dictated. Most of them would be despatched without revision. Is it any wonder then that some of them contain very long sentences; that some sentences are hardly grammatical. His passionate love for Christ made him sometimes express his ideas quicker than his secretary, Sylvanus, could jot them down. One of the problems that constantly angered him (and it recurs constantly in his letters) is that occasioned by a group of people called 'Judaizers'. The first Jewish converts to Christianity could not appreciate that their Jewish beliefs and laws were now superfluous. They wanted the Gentile converts first to accept the Jewish faith, the Jewish law and way of life, and only then to believe in Jesus. These

'Judaizers' dogged Paul's footsteps and tried to win over his converts to all the laws of the Jewish religion: to circumcision, to a recognition of clean and unclean foods, to fasting, and to strict Sabbath-keeping. Even after the matter was settled at the first Council in the Church (Acts 15) the difficulties continued.

THE LAW DOES NOT SAVE

The Jews had believed that it was the external keeping of the Law which saved them. This led inevitably to the self-righteousness of the Pharisees: 'I have kept the Law, therefore God is obliged to save me.' This is equivalent to saying, 'I can save myself. I am independent of God.' This is totally opposed to the Christian spirit. It is not the Law that saves: it is Christ Jesus who saves us. It is he who raised us up from our misery. 'Yet we know that a man is put right with God only through faith in Jesus Christ, never by doing what the Law requires . . . If a man is put right with God through the Law, it means that Christ died for nothing!' (Galatians 2:16, 21)

Paul was worried that the converts would begin to rely for salvation on external observances, whereas the power of Jesus' death-resurrection is the cause of our salvation. It is because of Jesus that there is now 'no difference between Jews and Gentiles, between slaves and free men, between men and women: you are all one in union with Christ Jesus.' (Galatians 3:28)

IN UNION WITH CHRIST JESUS

This phrase 'in union with Christ Jesus' (or its equivalent) occurs over two hundred times in Paul's letters. This is the key that opens the door to Paul's thought. In his letters to the Romans he writes:

> . . . when we were baptized into union with Christ

Jesus, we were baptized into union with his death. By our baptism, then, we were buried with him and shared his death, in order that, just as Christ was raised from death by the glorious power of the Father, so also we might live a new life. For if we became one with him in dying as he did, in the same way we shall be one with him by being raised to life as he was. (Romans 6:3-5)

This is the centre of Paul's faith: that Jesus is not just a hero from the past, nor even one who now lives but dwells in some inaccessible place. He is one who lives with us and in us by his Spirit today, here and now. This was the vision he had received on the road to Damascus. And he applies this belief to every problem. Is there a problem of impurity? How can you join your body, Paul asks, to the body of a prostitute, when you are already 'in Christ Jesus'? Is there a problem of disunity? Where there is dissension, let there be unity because we are all one 'in Christ Jesus'. The problem of a runaway slave? 'Now he is not just a slave, but much more than a slave: he is a dear brother in Christ', so please, Philemon, take him back without punishment.

For discussion

1. Can any member of the group recall any passage from one of St Paul's letters that has influenced him?
2. Paul's letters are mainly to do with the problems of his day. Does this mean that his letters have little to say to us today?
3. If Paul were writing a letter to the church at —————— (your diocese) what, in your opinion, would be the most pressing problem he would be writing about?
4. Here are a number of the most famous passages from St Paul's letters. Members of the group may care to

look them up and say what message emerges from them now.

Romans 8 : 12-30
1 Corinthians 13 : 1-10
Ephesians 3 : 14-20
Philippians 2 : 6-11

CHAPTER 10

Whatever Happened to the
Ten Commandments?

'The Ten Commandments don't seem to be taught in school these days. Things were stricter in the old days. People knew what the Ten Commandments were. Of course, they didn't always keep them, but when they broke them, they knew they had done wrong. But not now. I think that if you asked them, the majority of young people today wouldn't even know what the Ten Commandments were.'

'It's not the same now as it used to be. At one time, everything was clear-cut, black and white. This was a sin, that was not. To do this was a mortal sin. To do that was a venial.'

'There's no fear of God any more. Or fear of hell. It's all just "love your neighbour" these days. Nothing about "love thy God". Religion is all horizontal. Nothing vertical in it all. If you ask me, it's pretty well just humanitarianism.'

'And when it comes to bringing up children, parents who still believe in the old morality are at a great disadvantage. Their children simply say, "But all the others are allowed to do it. Why can't I?"'

In this chapter we are going to begin looking at the moral development of young people. 'Conscience formation' is another way of describing this process. Notice

those two words 'development' and 'formation'. Both
words imply a continuing activity. Our moral attitudes
and the decisions about behaviour that we make, develop (or rather *should* develop) as we grow older. It's
really all part of the process of growing up, of matur-
ing. The people who have stopped growing up are im-
mature. Morally, they are Peter Pans.

PEOPLE AROUND ME
Children are not born with a 'built-in' conscience. In
fact, one might say that there is no such thing as 'conscience' in that there is no special and separate faculty
which decides whether an action is right or wrong.
'Conscience' is in fact the judgement of my reason
regarding right and wrong; it is the awareness of myself
as a person in process of becoming related to God and
to others, with responsibilities towards both.

Naturally my judgement of right and wrong will be
swayed most of all by the judgements of those around
me, most especially those I love and look up to. In that
sense a young person's conscience is being formed
continually. Older people are less impressionable; their
moral attitudes have to some extent 'jelled'. But youngsters, more sensitive to all that happens about them,
almost inevitably adopt the moral standards of their
family and their friends.

A father was interviewed on Radio Merseyside. His
son had been in the juvenile court on a charge of stealing
ball-point pens from school. 'I just can't understand
it,' said the father. 'He had no need to steal pens and
pencils; I bring home lots of them from work.' Here we
have an example of the way in which the moral values
and standards of the home are quickly assumed by the
child.

THE TEN COMMANDMENTS

Let's deal with a few of the points raised in the conversation that opened this chapter. First of all, the commandments.

'Children today do not know the Ten Commandments. Why aren't the Ten Commandments taught in school any longer?' That's how the question was phrased in a recently published résumé of what is taught in Catholic primary schools.[1] The author's answer is as follows:

If what is said here were literally true, then indeed it would be a very serious matter and not only would the school be to blame but the parents likewise. I suspect, however, that what is meant is that many children cannot recite the Ten Commandments as we learnt them, and not that children do not know it is wrong to tell a lie or to steal or to be disobedient. Clearly, very many children do steal, do lie and are disobedient, but whether or not they do these things without knowing that they are wrong is a very different question.

The new approach does not insist that all the Ten Commandments be known by heart; it wants the children to know those Commandments which have immediate bearing upon their daily lives and it wants them to know these Commandments not in the 'DO NOT' form but in the positive form of, 'THIS IS HOW TO BEHAVE.' So from the early stages in the primary school the child is helped to know how he should behave by the following simplified forms of those Commandments which have some bearing upon his life:

Love God our Father;

Be kind and loving to each other;

Do what Mum and Dad tell you;

[1] *Step by Step* (Motherwell Religious Education Centre), p. 58.

Forgive each other;

Be truthful;

Be honest.

But what is much more important than giving children commandments to learn is to introduce the children to God as their Father and to Jesus as their brother and to help them to get to know the Father through Jesus. Jesus shows us all how to live as good children of our Father. Therefore there is really only one rule of life, 'Be like Jesus.' The children have to become the kind of person Jesus is. His life was marked continually by kindliness; he shared all that he had with others; he cared for others and he forgave others. These are the marks of Jesus, the Son of God, and should be the marks of all the children of God. It is well to remember that Jesus told us that all the Commandments can be summed up in the two great Commandments: 'Love God' and 'Love one another.' (Matthew 22:33-40)

LEADING TO FREEDOM

Our youngsters must be helped to look on the Commandments not as ten barbed-wire entanglements, inhibiting freedom. The Commandments are good not because God ordered them. God ordered them because what they command is good. The youngster must see the Commandments as promising freedom, not imprisonment; as leading to a fuller life, not a diminished one; as protecting all that is good in human relationships, not as a taking away of the joy of living.

Unfortunately, for some, the decalogue appears like a rather nasty test devised by God. If we eventually pass this test – then we earn heaven for ourselves! This view of salvation is first cousin to an ancient heresy – (old heresies never die; they just go marching on) – devised by an English (or possibly Irish) monk of the fifth century, named Pelagius. He cannot have been very familiar with St Paul's letters. We don't earn God's love or God's reward, says Paul.

'For it is by God's grace that you have been saved, through faith. It is not your own doing, but God's gift. There is nothing here to boast of, since it is not the result of your own efforts.' (Ephesians 2:8-9)

'If you believe,' says Paul in another letter, 'that keeping the law is going to earn your salvation, then Christ died for nothing.' (Galatians 2:21)

THE COMMANDMENTS DO MATTER BUT . . .
Jesus said, 'If you love me, you will obey my commandments.' (John 14:15) Notice the order of the words: love first, then the law. In other words, if you love a person, you will do what he wants you to do. Simply obeying Jesus' commandments will not lead you to love him. But having a personal, intimate and loving relationship with Jesus will lead you to ask what are the ways (commandments) by which you can demonstrate your love.

Love makes far greater demands on a person than the law. A nurse can do all that is demanded of her by the 'law' of the hospital in looking after patients. But if her husband is taken ill and needs nursing at home, her love for him will lead her to lose sleep and food and leisure, far in excess of anything she would be willing to endure, no matter how adequately, for patients in the hospital.

In other words, our young people's morality should be bound up with the love of God in Jesus Christ, rather than a list of commandments. The actor, Peter Cushing, was talking on television of the effects comics had on him as a child. He admitted that as a twelve-year-old his day-to-day behaviour was to a great extent modelled

on a hero from *Boy's Own Paper*. He would ask himself, 'Would Ricky' (I forget the actual name, but that
will do) 'behave in this way? Well, in that case, so will
I.' In a similar way, a youngster's moral decisions must
be linked to a person rather than a code of laws. And
that person is Jesus Christ.

WHERE HAS ALL THE FEAR GONE?

At one time it was thought proper to use the idea of hell
and eternal suffering to frighten people into religious
observance. Some people quote from the psalms – 'The
beginning of wisdom is the fear of the Lord.' But there
is fear and fear. There must be an *awe* of God – for awe
is the beginning of adoration, the most basic and indispensable of attitudes. You cannot frighten people into
loving God. And that is all that God our Father wants
from us – our love. Indeed that is why we must be free.
Morality and love are based on freedom. 'You can't buy
love,' so went the words of the song. Neither can you
force love. It must be freely offered. Fear of eternal
punishment may have led some people in the past to
abandon a life of sin. But to use fear now as a lever
would with most young people be quite ineffective.
Jesus told us a great deal about his Father, but never
once did he say that he was someone we should be
frightened of.

IT IS GOOD NEWS

In any case, Gospel means 'Good News'. Is it good news
if the preacher says, 'I'm going to tell you something
that's going to scare the daylights out of you'?

St Paul wrote:

>   . . . the Spirit that God has given you does not
> make you a slave and cause you to be afraid; instead,
> the Spirit makes you God's sons, and by the Spirit's

power we cry to God, Abba, Father. (Romans 8:15)

For the Spirit that God has given us does not make us timid; instead, his Spirit fills us with power, and love, and self-control. (2 Timothy 1:7)

St John similarly:

There is no fear in love; perfect love drives out all fear. So then, love has not been made perfect in the one who fears, because fear has to do with punishment. We love because God first loved us. (1 John 4:18-19)

HORIZONTAL VERSUS VERTICAL?

" 'You must love the Lord your God with all your heart, with all your soul, and with all your mind." This is the greatest and the most important commandment. The second most important commandment is like it: "You must love your fellow-man as yourself." The whole law of Moses [i.e. the commandments] and the teachings of the prophets depend on these two commandments.' (Matthew 22:37-40)

That is the way Jesus himself summed it up. There should be no conflict between our love for God and our love for our brethren.

St Paul was not contradicting this saying of Jesus when he wrote:

As for you, my brothers, you were called to be free. But do not let this freedom become an excuse for letting your physical desires rule you. Instead, let love make you serve one another. *For the whole Law is summed up in one commandment: 'Love your fellow-man as yourself.'* (Galatians 5:13-14 – author's italics)

There is no contradiction between Jesus' 'two' commandments and Paul's 'one' because in fact the only way in which we can express our love for God is through the love we show our brethren. Conversely, 'If a man is rich and sees his brother in need, yet closes his heart against his brother, how can he claim that he has love for God in his heart? . . . Our love should not be just words and talk; it must be true love, which shows itself in action.' (1 John 3:17-18)

A man cannot love God and not at the same time love his brethren. An atheist or an agnostic or a secular humanist, may love his brethren but not God. But is he to be blamed for having no faith in God? We are not to judge. And the Gospel would seem to rate *his* chances of salvation greater than those of the believer who said 'Lord, Lord,' but who shut his heart against his brethren.

SUMMING UP

The way children behave depends more on parents than anyone else. The child is not born with a 'built-in' conscience. His conscience is formed by the behaviour he sees about him, especially in the home.

It is not what parents *say* that leads a child to an understanding of what is right and wrong. It is what the parents really think and how they behave, and the attitudes the parents themselves display that will most affect their child.

The attitudes we would like our children to have:

Within the family – courtesy, respect, sympathy, tolerance, affection.

Outside the family – affection, respect, tolerance, honesty. Jesus said, 'Don't just be nice to those who are nice to you.'

Groups outside – Racial intolerance is extremely un-

Christian. Words such as 'Wog', 'Coon', 'Nigger', 'Yid', 'Packy' indicate racial intolerance.

About things – 'Giving is better than getting.' Children should be led to have sympathy for those who are less fortunate (especially those in the Third World). They should be encouraged towards an attitude of thankfulness for what they have. Honesty is most important yet difficult of achievement in a society which laughingly admits to 'borrowing', 'knocking off' and 'finding', but which would be horrified to be called 'thieving'.

The child must be helped to see the difference between an accident and a sin. He needs help to see why some actions are wrong and other actions desirable. Reasons for obedience should not depend upon the parents' 'Because I say so'.

We must not confuse 'sinful' with what is just annoying to us.

It is very puzzling to the child if parents are very strict one day, indifferent another, permissive another. We need to be consistent.

Nagging is counter-productive. Praise produces progress.

For discussion
1. Do members of the group feel that it is easier to be a Christian now than previously?
2. Is being a Christian supposed to be a soft option? Is there not something wrong with our understanding of Christianity, if adhering to it presents us with no difficulty?
3. Do you agree that love makes greater demands than law?
4. Are you of the opinion that young people today are

little concerned with the law but more concerned with making something positive of their lives?

5. Have members of the group seriously considered the demands on our Christian conscience of the needs of the Third World?

6. How do members of the group deal with the complaint sometimes made by older children: 'All the others are allowed to do it. Why can't I?'?

7. What do you understand by 'horizontal versus vertical'?

CHAPTER II

Maturity, Freedom and Happiness

'No parent wakes up in the morning planning to make his child's life miserable. No mother says to herself, "Today I'll shout, nag, and humiliate my child whenever possible." On the contrary, in the morning many mothers resolve: "This is going to be a peaceful day. No shouting, nor arguing, and no fighting." Yet, in spite of good intentions, the unwanted war breaks out again. Once more we find ourselves saying things we do not mean, in a tone we do not like.

'All parents want their children to be secure and happy. No one deliberately tries to make his child fearful, shy, inconsiderate, or objectionable. Yet in the process of growing up, many children acquire undesirable characteristics and fail to achieve a sense of security and an attitude of respect for themselves and for others. We want children to be polite and they are rude; we want them to be neat and they are messy; we want them to be self-confident and they are insecure; we want them to be happy and they are not.'[1]

In this chapter and the next we are going to look at the way children grow up. Not the way their bodies grow, nor the way they develop their reasoning powers — except indirectly. We are going to concern ourselves with the manner in which their moral attitudes develop. Of course, no two children are the same. Each

[1] *Between Parent and Child* by Dr Haim G. Ginott (Staples Press, 1969).

child is unique. So we mustn't think that the necessarily general statements that follow will exactly fit every child. However, the pattern described in this and the subsequent chapter is a fairly constant one.

LOVE AND SECURITY

No parent is in doubt of the child's need for love and security. These two allied felt states are the indispensable foundation for all development.

For it is generally true to say that our ability to love other people as we grow older is in proportion to the extent in which we were conscious of being loved ourselves when we were very young. Or to put it another way: a person who, as a small child, was deprived of love suffers from a most severe handicap. He will have to make a superhuman effort if he is to surmount it. Similarly the child who feels that he cannot trust his parents, who does not feel secure with them, will find it difficult later to trust anyone. 'If I can't trust my mum and dad, who can I trust?'

If a person is going to relate to others easily, it will depend more than anything else on his ability to love and trust them. In fact, one sure sign of maturity is the facility and speed with which a person can feel at home with others, and persuade others to feel at home with him. (That most mature of men, the man-God, Jesus Christ, had this skill in a pre-eminent degree. (Cf. John chapters 4 and 9, and many other places in the Gospels.)

SELF-ESTEEM

The most worthwhile action anyone can perform is to lead another person to value himself, to see his own worth. I would find it impossible to think of any way in which I could better help another person than by helping him to respect himself, yes, to love himself. For he will never be able to love anyone else, if he hasn't first been able to love himself.[2] 'Man . . . must love his neighbour as himself,' said Jesus (Mark 12:33). '. . . We do not receive enough love in our early years to have an adequate self-evaluation or the ability to give ourselves fully in love to others . . . If we must accept ourselves before we can effectively love others, we also understand that love for others is essentially a campaign to build their self-esteem.'[3]

While no one would dispute that the moral development of the child demands that he is sure that he is loved, some parents are confused as to how they may reassure the child that he is indeed loved. 'Does it mean that we have always to be giving in to him?' some ask. Or, 'Have we to convince him of our love by the toys and presents we buy him?' That is not the way. The proof of our love lies elsewhere. It lies in the effort parents are willing to make in letting the lives of their children and themselves intertwine. With very young children this will consist largely in play, in fondling, in talk. With older children, it will show itself very largely in listening and talking – two thirds listening, one third talking!

HAPPY TALK

Conversation with children (not talking down) is good for many reasons. It convinces them that parents, and older brothers and sisters, love them. It also extends their vocabulary – an indispensable tool to learning and expression. It helps them to value prayer – only if children have seen the joy of talking with parents they

[2] This is not to dispute the necessity for self-discipline. But self-discipline is not self-denigration which is little more than masochism. I discipline myself *because* I love myself.

[3] *Life for a Wanderer* by Andrew Greeley (Image Books, 1971).

can see, will they place any value in talking with a Father in heaven whom they can't see. Conversation with parents also contributes greatly to the mental and emotional health of the child. Parents by listening and talking can act as a mirror to a child's emotions. This in fact is the art of counselling. Counselling does not mean offering advice. Rather the counsellor simply attempts to help the 'client' to clarify his emotions. The client in need of counselling (in this case the child) sees things out of focus; his emotions have distorted the projected image of himself. The counsellor (in this case the parent) helps the child refocus reality.

Dr Haim, in the book already referred to, gives an example of this:

Ten-year-old Harold came home grumpy and complaining.

Harold: What a miserable life! The teacher called me a liar, just because I told her that I forgot my homework. And she shouted. My goodness, did she shout! She said she'll write you a note.

Mother: You had a very rough day.

Harold: You can say that again.

Mother: It must have been terribly embarrassing to be called a liar in front of the whole class.

Harold: Yes, it was.

Mother: I bet inside yourself you called her a few names!

Harold: Oh, yes! But how did you know?

Mother: That's what we generally do when someone hurts us.

Harold: That's a relief.

'The function of an emotional mirror,' Dr Haim concludes, 'is to reflect feelings as they are, without distortion:

' "It looks as though you are very angry."

' "It sounds as if you hate him very much."

' "It seems that you are disgusted with the whole set-up."

'To a child who has such feelings, these statements are most helpful. They show him clearly what his feelings are. Clarity of image, whether in a looking glass or in an emotional mirror, provides opportunity for self-initiated grooming and change.'

LOVE IS NOT POSSESSIVE

True love wants the well-being of the other for the other's sake, not for his own sake, whether for enjoyment or pride of possession. Genuine love is never possessive. Yet we have to face the fact that there is a tendency in us all to want those we love to be little replicas of ourselves. We want them to see things the way we do, have the same likes and dislikes. Whereas, the one who truly loves another equivalently says : 'I'm glad you are you. I love you because you are you.'

I believe that this tendency in us all to attempt to possess those we love is a hazard that we must face honestly. It shows itself in different ways : one of its symptoms is overprotectiveness. This invariably stunts the child's growth towards maturity. Indeed one can soon identify the adult whose childhood has been spent under the tutelage of parents who were overprotective.

BE DISPENSABLE

The good parent is one who aims at making himself dispensable. He sees that the young person must increasingly make decisions for himself. For example in buying clothes, mother may well know best when it comes to a general selection of a number of options, but in the final choice of a particular 'buy', it is good for even the young child to make his own choice. People act responsibly when they are treated as responsible. (Complaints are made about the 'irresponsible behaviour' of some sections of workers in industry. But can one expect responsible behaviour from people who are treated as unthinking zombies and accorded absolutely no responsibility beyond the repetition of a few simple actions along the assembly line?)

MATURITY AND FREEDOM

Growing towards maturity is a growth towards the right use of freedom. Indeed the history of God's dealing with men is a story of God beckoning people towards freedom. Unfortunately, the Ten Commandments are commonly regarded as prohibitions, as ten curbs on a person's freedom. But that is not God's way of thinking. The Bible prefaces the giving of the Commandments with these words:

> I am Yahweh your God who brought you out of the land of Egypt, *out of the house of slavery*. (Exodus 20:1 – Author's italics)

God wants men to be free because he wants their love and love can never be forced. Hence, it is not surprising that we find the same concern shown by God in the Old Testament that men should be free to respond in love or not, reflected also in the New Testament in the life and teaching of Jesus. 'And you, would you like to leave also?' said Jesus to his apostles, when many of his followers left him. Not, 'I hope you aren't going to leave me also.' The rich young man who couldn't face the sacrifice 'went away sad'. Jesus did not call him back with either promises or threats.

The story of the prodigal son 'is the story of a teenager, a typical teenager. He has an affluent home, and a father far from heavy-handed. But he feels that urge to grow, to be himself, no longer his father's son but himself. It is a natural and commendable call. And this unusual father knows his younger boy. He knows this son finds the farm oppressive and the life narrow. The elder son is so different; steady, rural, reliable. But no two sons are alike and the father is aware that this younger and impetuous son must be allowed his head, must be given his freedom, which will entail the freedom to make mistakes, let him try the *dolce vita*, let him seek salvation in the secular city, let him live and learn. A usual son. An unusual father.'[4]

SUMMING UP

To sum up this chapter: humanly speaking, the child's image of God and the sort of relationship he has with God, will have been mediated very largely through his parents and the relationship he has with them. In general, it would be true to say:

If his parents are exacting, demanding, perfectionists, then the child's God will be one who is demanding, exacting, a perfectionist.

If his parents are loving, then his God will be a loving God.

If he feels secure with his parents, then his God will be one in whom he trusts completely.

If his parents are unyielding, unforgiving, then he will find it hard to believe that God is forgiving.

If his parents fail to support him in all situations, then he will come to believe that God is against him — a belief held by a vast number of Christians to whom God appears as someone to be placated, automatically opposing them until appeased by some good deed.

[4] From an article by Fr Hugh Lavery in the *Sower*, July 1973.

If his parents show their continual support and concern, he will more easily believe that God is on his side.

If he finds that his parents are not particularly interested in what he has to say, then he will almost certainly find it hard to believe that God listens to his prayer.

If he finds it enjoyable to talk to his parents, because he is aware that they are genuinely interested in what he has to say, he will believe that God is a loving Father, to whom also he will want to talk.

If he sees that his parents, while intensely interested in all he does, and by no means permissive of bad behaviour, nevertheless allow him freedom of choice, he will more easily come to look on God, not as someone who restricts his freedom, but as one who wants him to be free to develop the personality that God has given him.

For discussion

1. Can members of the group recognize characteristics in themselves, and attitudes towards God, which they now possess because of the outlook of their parents?

2. Have you any experiences you can share which may help other parents in the group carry out most effectively their role as 'counsellor' to their children. If there should be any teenage children in the group, what suggestions can they offer?

3. What difficulties stand in the way of conversation with one's children? With one's parents? Are the members of the group convinced of its value?

4. 'The good parent is one who aims at making himself dispensable.' Examples?

5. One parent has said: 'If you mistrust your children, or suspect them of some moral misdemeanour, very

often the mistrust and suspicion seem to drive the youngsters into doing the very thing about which you mistrusted them.' Any comments on this?

6. What difference is there between freedom and permissiveness?

CHAPTER 12

See How They Grow

In this chapter we are going to look at four young people:

  Moira aged six and a half
  Frankie aged ten
  Barbara aged fourteen
  Alan aged sixteen

CONSCIOUSLY IMITATING

Moira has had a fortunate start in life. She knows that her parents really love her. This gives her confidence and self-assurance. She has a fairly big vocabulary – about 2500 words – this is because her parents talk with her a great deal. She has also caught the 'reading' habit from them. Because she is so young, each experience now makes a deeper impression than it will later. These are the magic years, the years of 'let's pretend'. Her vivid imagination can visualize goblins and fairies in the pattern of the wallpaper. She can talk to an invisible friend. Animals can speak. Her doll really cries.

She wants her parents' approval above all else. She tries to 'keep the rules' so that she won't lose this approval. Her judgements about what is right and what is wrong depend entirely on what she is told. Her behaviour is continually being modelled on the behaviour around her – especially that of her parents whom she is consciously imitating.

She can't yet figure out motives. Nor does she understand the difference between doing something wrong on

purpose (such as smashing a plate in a fit of temper) and an accident (such as letting three plates slip when she's helping with the washing up). In fact if the latter caused more of a rumpus than the former – then she will regard the second as the greater crime. (See also footnote on p. 156.)

CONSISTENCY

One important help that Moira has received is that her parents are consistent over 'rules'. Some parents are strict one day, indifferent another day, and 'anything goes' on a third. This is most confusing to young children. It's not this way with Moira's parents who try to be the same with her all the time. She feels secure because she knows what behaviour they expect of her.

Another advantage she's had is that her mother and father are in the habit of explaining the reasons for the things they ask her to do or not do. When she asks, 'But why can't I, Mummy?' she doesn't get a curt reply, 'Because I say so, see.' With patience her mother tries to give the reasons why she should or should not do certain things.[1] This makes the motive for obedience *internal* to the child. Obedience will thus not depend upon the presence of someone *external* who may or may not always be around.

SHELL OF SELF

Very young children are by nature and of necessity very egocentric. It would be unnatural for them to be otherwise. They are the centre of their own world. Moira is just beginning to break out of this shell of egocentricity. She knows when she does wrong. She is sorry afterwards if her tantrums have upset the peace

[1] Yes, I know Moira's parents are saints. So are the parents of Frankie, Barbara, and Alan.

of home. She was very apologetic after she had
scratched Susan's face in a fit of temper. (Susan had
pushed her pram over.) Later she went next door and
very shamefacedly apologized to Susan and her parents.
'Now you must say sorry to God,' her mother said to
her later and was surprised when Moira answered,
'Why should I? I didn't scratch his face.' Nevertheless
she did say, 'I'm sorry, dear God my Father' – but
whether this was because her mother told her to, or
because she realized that somehow her temper had
offended God, God alone knows. No one else.

THINKING CONCRETELY

It need hardly be said that Moira can think only in concrete individual terms. If a slice of bread, an orange, a
banana, a meat-pie, an egg, were put in front of her and
she were asked, 'What are all these things?' she would
not be able to say, 'They are all things you eat.' Very
likely she would point to each item and give it its name.
If the question were repeated, she might point out the
colour of each. In the same way she's not able to
classify her actions – she cannot say, 'I have disobeyed
six times,' though she might be able to describe six
separate actions. Even this however would be unlikely
as her memory for transient actions will go back little
farther than this morning. Abstract words such as
goodness, peace, joy, justice, truth, are merely sounds
in her ears. They mean almost nothing to her.

MAGIC YEARS

Frankie, our ten-year-old, is not happy playing on his
own (as Moira is). His friends are beginning to be, in one
sense, more important to him than even his parents.
  The fairy-tale age has ended. Now the action-packed
real-life *Swiss Family Robinson* type of story is the one

that appeals to him. Although 'fairies' are passé, magic is not. This has its dangers as far as religion is concerned. 'I say these words and, hey presto, all my sins are gone' – this is the sort of attitude he could easily assume towards sorrow for sin, and confession.

Whereas a younger child can be motionless and wonder at things (a type of contemplation), Frankie is utterly unable to keep still unless he is very interested in a story, or is finding out about things – his curiosity is insatiable – or making things. He's very much an extrovert. He is easily bored with prayers, because he has to keep still, and often doesn't disguise his disinterest in church, except on those occasions when he is either serving or bringing the offertory gifts to the altar. His mother and father often have to correct him but they are careful to point out the *why* of the wrongdoing rather than the mere fact of it. Because of his involvement with his peers, he is able to appreciate the idea that no sin is entirely a private affair. It hurts the other members of God's family.

LITTLE LEGALIST

Even so, Frankie is very legalistically minded. He believes in the letter of the law rather than the spirit. 'But Mum, you told me not to take Sandy's jig-saw. Well I didn't. I just took his model aeroplane.' 'I didn't pull Melanie's pony-tail. I just took hold of it and she ran off.' For this reason his parents are finding it hard to help Frankie realize that sin is much more than the breaking of a law. It damages the friendship between himself and his Friend, Jesus.

He can be hard on other children and insensitive to compassion for others (unless his parents point out the need for compassion and show it themselves). This is the age not only for 'ganging up' but also for excluding newcomers from the gang. However, he is extremely sensitive over 'fair play', and is aggrieved at what he considers unjust treatment. In fact he finds this the only thing hard to forgive.

Every now and again, Frankie's parents and teachers pat themselves on the back and say, 'At last, he's beginning to behave like a Christian.' But then, suddenly, all moral advancement seems to vanish and he appears to be just a little savage. The road to maturity and freedom is indeed long and hard.

ABOUT BARBARA

Dear Frances,

I felt very relieved when I got your letter this morning suggesting that Barbara might stay with you for a few weeks during the holidays. I am sure she will be glad to have Anne's company; they are both fourteen, nearly fifteen.

I must tell you that she has been a real trial to us in the last few months: moody, sulky, sometimes hardly speaking to us; at other times, but for very short spells, noisily happy. Usually she seems to be more contented when she's with other people. It's us, her own mother and father, it seems she can't be bothered with. At times she gives the impression of wanting to be independent; and at other times she reverts to being almost a child again. One day she seems almost to flaunt her figure, which is now becoming more womanly. The next day she seems to want to disguise the fact that she's growing up.

She got a rather poor report from school. From what I can gather all her class did. When her father and I tried to talk it over with her, she flew into a temper. Told us that we had never understood her. Then she said something that hurt us deeply. 'It's all this religion you've been ramming down my throat,' she shouted. 'I'm fed up with religion. I don't believe a word of it. I'm never going to pray again. I've finished with all that God-stuff.'

I don't know what you will decide to do about her going with you to church while she's at your house. We leave her very much to her own devices on a Sunday morning. We came to the conclusion that to force her to accompany us to Mass would reinforce her mood of rebellion. Actually I was glad to hear, quite accidentally, that she had joined a group of friends and she goes to St John's where they have a very friendly and lively Mass, not always 'folk', but there is coffee afterwards and records in the hall. The sermon is not long and the priest isn't a prophet of gloom. Seems quite happy himself and makes the congregation welcome.[2]

Anyway it's over to you for the next three weeks, and the best of luck! If you want we could have your daughter, Anne, back to stay with us either at Christmas time or next summer. However, I ought to say that Harry and I have come to the conclusion that we are not very good parents if our effect on Barbara is anything to go by.

With all good wishes,

Angela

Dear Angela,

Thank you for your letter about Barbara. We are delighted to have her. I must tell you that since coming here she has been quite the opposite of what you led me to expect: charming, helpful, cheerful. And you should

---

[2] Karl Rahner in *The Priesthood* tells of a mother who on her death bed drank a glass of champagne with her priest son and then said: 'Go home now and sleep well, and I shall sleep into eternity. Don't look too sad about it. If priests look sad, nobody believes what they say.'

see how motherly she is with our nine-year-old! I can't
say that I was altogether surprised at the transformation
because, as you know, Anne's elder sister, now nineteen,
went through exactly the same phase. Bolshy, sulky,
bad-tempered, and so on. The same thing happens with
boys as well except that they go through this awkward
phase usually about a year later than girls.

What they are trying to do at this stage of their lives
is to find an identity for themselves. At times they are
very insecure, at other times very sure of themselves.
They swing back and forth between these two extremes.
Hence the moodiness.

I'm sure you are following the right policy: great
patience and tolerance. There's no point in nagging. No
point in saying, 'Snap out of it.' You can't snap out of a
transitional stage of development that's going to last
more than a year.

As far as religion is concerned, you've surely hit the
right note. No duress – no sermonizing. Just patience
and affection.

This state of growth is as painful for us parents as it
is for the youngsters. Dick and I sometimes wish that
they were all off our hands for good, safely married.
Then we realize that in the Darby and Joan club we'll
only have memories.

Here's to September,
Affectionately,
Frances

TEMPORARY HAVEN

Alan, aged sixteen, has arrived at a calm haven after the
storms of the previous years. 'The vulnerable strivings
towards independence [of earlier adolescence] have
turned into a calm feeling of emancipation. There is

a more stable outlook towards the future.'[3] He has reached a peak plateau of intellectual activity – it will never be higher than now. Emotionally Alan is sensitive to the needs of others. Of course he is preoccupied with exams, but he is also wondering to what sort of social use he will be able eventually to apply his talents.

He doesn't find himself attracted to follow in his father's footsteps. In one frank moment he expressed it like this: 'I'm very grateful to you for everything you've done for me. I know I'm very lucky to have lived in such a comfortable home. But I must tell you that the people of my generation generally don't dig the idea of just getting a safe job that will keep the cog-wheels of capitalism running smoothly. There's more to life than just trying to buy a semi-detached, getting married, and working in the office from 9 to 5. You know that song "Little Boxes" – well that's my genera-tion's signature tune. At least that's the way I feel right now. In a few years time I may change . . . but I don't think I will.'

Some of Alan's contemporaries do voluntary social work.[4] Alan himself is seriously considering the possi-bility of Voluntary Service Overseas. He seems to hold in low esteem the consumer creature-comforts the pre-vious generation found irresistible. It could be because he didn't have to strive for them as his parents did. It

[3] *The Psychology of Childhood and Adolescence* by C. I. Sandström (Pelican Books, 1968), p. 222.

[4] Alan may not be altogether typical, but an increasing number of young people from committed Christian homes think and feel this way. If he had come from a home where a completely materialistic outlook prevailed, he might have grown into an unprincipled young man, a cynic and a savage disguising himself beneath a veneer of polite behaviour. Any children he might have fathered would be likely to become the petty monsters forecast in *A Clockwork Orange*.

could also be because he is more acutely aware than his parents are that a quarter of the world's population goes to bed hungry every evening.

Alan doesn't automatically respect people in authority. They need to earn his approval. To his parents' regret, the laws of the church cut no ice with him, unless he is convinced that they make sense. He goes to church, not because of the law, but because he wants to. He refuses to go to his own parish. 'I would rather go to a church where the Gospel comes over as Good News. Where the priest doesn't concentrate in his sermon on the remote past and the remote future, but speaks about life now.'

Alan is on the way towards moral maturity. His view of life is unprejudiced. He won't make snap judgements on people. He accepts people as they are. Most of his decisions are altruistic – that is, they are determined largely by the needs of his fellow men.

His parents are proud of him – but a little fearful. He seems much freer than they were at his age; much less 'tied' to his Church, more open towards people of other faiths, and indeed people of no religious faith. All that he asks is that they be sincere, be their genuine selves, refuse to put on an act. He just cannot tolerate the phoney. Genuineness in people is more important to him than the denominational labels they may pin on themselves.

'If only he could meet a good Christian girl,' his parents say wistfully to each other. But Alan keeps his own counsel.

For discussion
1. Are these four characters recognizable to members of the group? (Please confine the discussion to each one in turn.)

2. If members of the group have children of First Confession and Communion age — would they discuss the signs in their children of readiness for these sacraments?

3. What about sex education? By whom? When? Telling what?

4. What about Alan? The strength of his position? The weaknesses?

CHAPTER 13

I Confess

A SURVEY

An accountant: You ask me about my confessional practice. I have to admit, I don't go as often as I used to. I can't quite pinpoint the reason. I think it may have something to do with the way I confess. It seems somewhat childish. It hasn't changed much since I first started.

A wife: My habits over the years haven't changed at all. I go to confession every month. I say more or less the same thing each time. The priest gives me an identical penance. It's a routine I have never questioned.

A priest: My dilemma about confession is that I either know my prospective confessor too well so that I hesitate to reveal my troubles to him, or else I don't know him well enough to trust that he will be able to help me in a sympathetic way. I want something more than absolution. Yet I don't want him to growl at me. I haven't resolved this difficulty. I am very dissatisfied with the situation.

A shop-assistant: I haven't been to confession since I left school. I'm getting married next year. I'll go to confession before then. I dread the prospect, but I believe in it.

A teacher: I'm that rare bird – a recent convert. The priest who instructed me was very helpful. I go for a chat with him every few weeks. I tell him my troubles and he listens extremely patiently. He seems not to be in any hurry to see the back of me. I try *not to keep him too long. He sometimes gives me advice, sometimes just makes sympathetic noises. Invariably I end by telling him in what ways I've been selfish with God and with my brethren. He suggests something useful that I might do as a penance. Usually it's related to my sins. He assures me of God's pardon and power by his absolution. I feel completely renewed.*

A college student: Has anyone ever published a Good Confessor Guide?

We all know that *in theory* confession should not be burdensome: that it is not like the paying of a civil fine after a legal misdemeanour; as we leave the confessional we should not be thinking, 'Well if I drop dead tonight He couldn't catch me out': that it should rather be the joyful reuniting of friends whose relationship has been strained or broken: that it is our meeting with Jesus today, an occasion on which, through our faith, we let him change our lives, make us more free, more happy. But in practice . . .

In practice, for most people, it is something very different.

THE MEMORY LINGERS ON

Before writing another word of this chapter, I must make a public confession about my confessions. I know I should have a different attitude, but the sad fact is that I do not in any sense relish the prospect of confessing. I sometimes ask myself if it could be due to the fact that my early confessions were fright-full? I can still remember vividly the smell of the confessional, a mixture of snuff and incense. I am still able to see the blue cotton curtain across the grille wafting ghost-like, and I recall the feeling of claustrophobia as I shut myself in the little box-like, darkened room. Even now I can hear the (unintentionally) unsympathetic grunts of the unseen priest as he acknowledged my nonsense sins.

The impressions of early childhood are the ones that bite the deepest. Could all those scary memories be the reason why today I, in common with many others, can't escape a feeling of unease towards this, the most merciful and consoling of sacraments? However, before we go on to discuss the Sacrament of Penance, let's look again at baptism.

BAPTISM TAKES

The advert read: 'Have your own herb garden. Send 50p and we will mail you 5 peat pots, each containing different herb seeds – Thyme, Sage, Marjoram, Fennel and Angelica. They will begin to grow as soon as you apply water.'

Funny how your mind works. The advert reminded me immediately of baptism. In a way baptism works in the opposite direction. You baptize the baby with water at the beginning of its life but it's only some years later that the baptism springs into life. For perhaps two, three, four, five or more years, baptism is dormant like the seed in utterly dry soil. It's only when the growing child becomes aware of God and of other people that by a decision 'for God', the baptism 'takes'.

FAMILY SERVING THE WORLD

We Christians have been baptized by water. But there are plenty of other people who haven't been and yet who are just as truly the children of God as we are. 'God wills that all men are saved' and 'God has no favourites' – both these quotations from the Bible would not allow us to believe otherwise. Every man, woman and child is counted 'in' unless and until they opt out.

Let's hope no one opts out.

If God is the Father of all, what then does baptism do for us? The ceremonies of baptism, and later of confirmation, mark us out to be members of a community dedicated, as Jesus Christ was, to the service of men and the world.

SET-BACKS AND UPSETS

It would be nice to think that once we had become aware of God as our Father, of Jesus as our Brother and Friend, and of the Spirit uniting us to Jesus, there would be no looking back; that our relationship with the three Persons – endorsed by the way we treated the people around us – would grow and deepen without a set-back. But, as they say, 'Human nature being what it is', this is not so. Just as there are occasional rows and upsets in even the most ideal marriage, so too in our relationship with the Godhead, there are times when we put ourselves and our own wishes in first place.

THE NEED TO CONFESS

We need to apologize. And the normal means for us is through the Sacrament of Penance. Some people say: 'Why do I need to confess to a priest? Why can't I just tell God I'm sorry and leave it at that?' The reason is this – any wrong-doing of which we are guilty harms the Body of Christ, that is, the whole community of Christians. I need to apologize not only to God my Father but to the community. The deputy of the community is the priest, delegated by the bishop to act in the name of the community.

LESS CONFESSING?

Some say that less people are going to confession nowadays. I wonder if this is true. My guess would be that the same number are going but they are confessing less frequently. Why should this be, if, as everyone recognizes, frequent confession is a good thing? Could it be that the manner of confessing, which many people have been unable to change as they grew older, is making confession less helpful?

It's one of the characteristics of human nature that we should want to share our troubles and our guilt with others. We all need from time to time to unburden ourselves. If a person feels unable to talk freely in confession, and is unable to move away from reciting a list of sins, one cannot be surprised if he confesses less frequently. He would like confession to cease being two consecutive monologues – his own followed by the priest's – and become a dialogue between two human beings of flesh and blood. But the confessional manner of a life-time is hard to discard. How to overcome this difficulty? To answer that question we need to look again at our idea of sin.

According to the law of our Church, Roman Catholics are *obliged* to confess all certain mortal sins. If one has not committed a mortal sin, not one single person, from the Pope downwards, can demand that one go to confession. It should be said also that it would be considered a grave crime by the Church if a priest were to refuse anyone Holy Communion (unless he be a public and notorious sinner) simply because he had not first confessed.[1]

MORTAL SIN REVISITED

Now a mortal sin is not the sort of thing one does unthinkingly. It's a most serious turn-about in one's life. It's a U-turn away from One who has hitherto been

[1] I am not talking here of the *advisability* of frequent confession, but simply of the *obligation* of confessing at all.

I Confess   111

regarded as a loving Father. It's like an act of treachery between one friend and another that would put an end to that friendship. It's like the decision of a husband or a wife to be divorced. Could it be that in the past we have 'cheapened' the notion of mortal sin, so that people have come to regard it as an easy thing 'to slip into'?

If that is so, are we left with 'only venial sins'? Not quite. There are surely such actions as would merit the title 'serious sin'. This sort of sin

. . . is comparable to a severe quarrel between a husband and wife. As outrageous as this quarrel might be, there is no thought and no expression of divorce even mentioned. In spite of everything, they still remain together in the same house. So with God. As serious as grave sin might be, the relationship between God and the sinner, like the married couples', is still intact. It has not been completely broken.

For the average good person grave sin is the un-rhythmed and freely done sin that was committed without undue influence. It is an isolated act with full consent and full knowledge; it demands confession. Isolated as it is, however, it is not a determining factor, by itself, for eternal damnation. That final punishment is the result of a general pattern, not a single act.[2]

[2] *It Is the Lord* by William Bausch (Fides Publishers, 1970). The same point is made by Ladislas Orsy in *Worship* (July 1973). 'We understood sin in the categories of mortal and venial sin. If it was not fatal, it was venial, i.e., hardly more than the refusal of a small gift of grace through a misguided act or omission. Those categories are insufficient for a new understanding. We need a new category to express the existence of a dangerous movement that contains a ruinous element, although it has not brought about a disaster yet. The person is still in communion with the church; he is in communion with God; but evil forces at work in his heart may lead him to the

LACK OF FREEDOM

The author of the book from which the above quotation is taken goes on to make a further important observation which should console those who are plagued with long-enduring habits.

> There is such a thing as a rhythmed, habit-pressured act pushing up through one's over-all love pattern. And this is not grave sin and maybe no sin at all. This is the act which is not a grave sin, not because it is not serious, but because in the person's psychological make-up, it is so strong as to normally overcome free consent (one of the essential conditions for sin). We can spot cases like this by simply noticing that, on the one hand, the person's over-all context of the love of God is very pervasive and, on the other hand, the force of the habit is strong. In other words, a person's over-all living is quite moral and christian, but he or she has a recurrent moral problem which distresses him and which he works hard to overcome. In spite of this, the force of habit is so strong as to overcome his resolutions. In cases like these we would have objectively grave wrong-doing but not necessarily grave sin because of the lack of freedom in the person. This is what the theologians

---

destruction of God's love within him. Whatever the name for such a false movement is to be, a Christian who is involved in it needs no reconciliation, since no break has taken place, but he needs healing, since he is sick.

'We experience difficulties in describing this predicament since internal desires, trends and movements are much more difficult to categorize than external actions. Should we call it a *seriously sinful* situation that does not amount to mortal sin? It is certainly more than what is generally understood by venial sin. At any rate, it is a sickness for which a remedy is needed. This remedy we see in communal penance, through which the life course of a person is readjusted by the grace of repentance in and with the community and by sacramental absolution.'

have always called the force of passion lessening the freedom of responsibility.

Examples might be drinking, masturbation, temper etc. Such acts for the faithful Christian are not generally grave sins (although they can be on occasion) and do not need confession as such, since conquering such wrong-doing, full knowledge or full consent might be missing. As I've said, the over-all pattern of a well-lived life is a proof that passion, not deliberation, is at work here. In a word, no one can have a strong, over-all love of God and still be breaking in a profound way his relationship with the Father several times a week!

ALL THE DIFFERENCE

We have discussed the obligation of confessing mortal sin and noted the fact that grave sin 'demands confession' of the sincere Catholic. What of the person who is not conscious of having failed in either of those ways? Is there any point in his confessing? Certainly there is. But confession should not be allowed to become a mechanical action, simply a matter of habit, the replaying of a well-worn disc.

Instead of merely confessing isolated actions, one might try to describe one's predominant failing. This is rather like the difference between saying 'I have broken my wrist' and 'I am suffering from a broken wrist.'

'I have hardly once spoken with God as a son should speak with a loving Father' is very much better than 'I have missed my night prayers ten times.'

'I am less and less interested in showing affection to my wife and find myself toying with the idea of a casual affair with a girl at work' is much more authentic than 'I have had lustful desires every day.'

TOTAL DEPENDENCE

This manner of confessing is more realistic for several reasons: it helps the penitent to analyse his weaknesses more thoroughly, and getting things off his chest in this manner is in itself psychologically therapeutic. Such a confession reminds him of his need for God's mercy and God's power on which he must rely totally if he is to become more fully a son of God. This, it seems to me, is what Christianity is all about. Once we admit, 'All right, Father God, I realize it now. I can do nothing of myself. I am a sinner and I need your pardon. I depend utterly on you,' then our salvation is at hand.

Finally, confessing in this manner allows the confessor some scope in giving advice and encouragement. One might also hope that the confessor will be able to give a penance suited to the confession, rather than a mere repetition of prayers a number of times.

WHAT TO DO

Let's suppose that you, the reader, are dissatisfied with your present manner of confessing; that for this reason you are celebrating this sacrament less and less frequently, yet find the prospect of making a more informal, a more casual and conversational type of confession daunting, what are you to do? Here are some suggestions:

1. Find a confessor whom you believe will be sympathetic to a non-recitation type of confession.
2. Take another look at the way you review your life before confession. Are you wedded to a method of 'examination of conscience' that has changed hardly at all over the years? Could it be that you are not concentrating enough on things you have omitted to do? The first question we should surely ask ourselves is, 'How have I used the talents God has given me?'

You may perhaps need to use a book for this part of your preparation for confession.[8]

3. If having taken steps 1 and 2 you still feel diffident, then when you enter the confessional, simply say to the confessor, 'I'm tired of the way I've been confessing. I would like to talk to you but I'm not quite sure how . . .'

For discussion

1. Comments, please, on the 'survey' at the start of this chapter.
2. Why should confession be like 'the joyful reuniting of friends'?
3. Have members of the group memories of early confessions that throw light on their present attitudes? What about young children today?
4. How do one's private sins hurt the whole community of Christ?
5. Can the members of the group share their experience of the manner in which they 'review their life' in preparation for confession?

[8] Some people have told me that they have been reluctant to buy the *Catholic Prayer Book* (Darton, Longman 1970), because the examination of conscience is too comprehensive!

CHAPTER 14

I Beg Your Pardon

Jack: St Joseph didn't build the first confessional in his carpenter's shop, you know.

Don: What do you mean? I don't get you.

Jack: Just that it would be hard to find a reference to confession in the first three hundred years of the Church's existence.

Don: Are you trying to tell me that the whole business of confessing one's sins was made up by priests a long time after Christ's death and resurrection?

Jack: I'm not trying to tell you that at all. The Church has always been aware of its power to forgive sins in the name of God. All I'm trying to say is that no sacrament has changed more over the centuries in the way it's been celebrated than this one. Did you know, for example, that at first it was believed that forgiveness of sin was a once-for-all-time thing? People in the early days believed that so strong was your call by baptism to share your life with Christ, you just weren't expected ever to renegue. But if you did, then you had only one chance left – forgiveness in the name of God and the Church by the bishop. If and when you had used up that one chance, you'd not have another.

Don: That was pretty severe.

Jack: And the penances they got in those days were severe too. They might be told to go to the Holy Land on pilgrimage. That would have taken them years. A diet of bread and water for the whole of Lent would have been considered quite moderate!

Don: It would hardly encourage people to come to confession.

Jack: It didn't. Quite a lot of people, when they had sinned grievously, would postpone reconciling themselves with God and the community until they were on their death bed.

Don: I suppose they knew then that they wouldn't be able to do the penance. How long did people keep on thinking of confession in that way?

Jack: The change came slowly. It was the Irish monks who introduced a manner of confessing more in line with that of our own time. This was about the year 500 plus.

Don: It must have been an improvement on what had gone on before. Did people like the new way?

Jack: Of course. But at first the authorities in the Church didn't. In fact a local council of bishops condemned it. But the practice just continued. The only difference between then and later was that the penance had to be completed *before* absolution was given, not after.

Don: And were the penances any easier?

Jack: Not much. But unfortunately some abuses crept in – you could get other people to do your penance for you!

Don: And when did the sacrament evolve into a form we would recognize today?

Jack: About four or five hundred years ago.

Don: Well, it's a big improvement on what it was like at first.

Jack: In some ways, perhaps. But the celebration of the sacrament lost a lot when it became divorced from the community.

Don: I don't understand you.

Jack: Well, for the first thousand years of the Church's existence, people couldn't help but see that it was not just a matter of getting *God's* forgiveness.

Don: I'm still not with you.

Jack: Every sin we commit affects the health of the Body of Christ of which we are all members. So if I do wrong, it's never just a private matter between God and me. The ceremony of reconciliation they held in the early days of the Church made this quite clear. But now it's just a few words whispered anonymously in a sort of spiritual launderette. You know how it is in launderettes. People are quite oblivious of each other. Never speak. They just sit there looking at their own dirty washing. Well, that's how it's been in our life-time, hasn't it, at confession on a Saturday night? Just God and me and my rotten, petty sins.

Don: It's hard to see how else it could be unless we had public confession.

Jack: There'll never be public confession. But there will be more public services of penance. In fact some parishes have them regularly now.

Don: And what's the effect?

Jack: Once they understand what the service is all about, people like them. They say the readings and hymns and prayers are very helpful. After all, in one way, when we sin, we may well be leading others to sin. It's only right that in our reconciliation with God and our brethren we should also help each other. By our sins we break the community down. It's only right that by a service such as this we should build our community up.

The worst thing of all would be if we Christians lost a sense of sin and lost the sense of a need for continuing conversion. If the decline in confession-

going is due to people losing their sense of sin and
their feeling of need for pardon and gratitude for
forgiveness, then God help us!

Don: Perhaps it could be that we in our age have
reached another turning-point in the history of confession. Maybe two people in 500 years, talking together as we are now, will say, 'The celebration of
this sacrament changed direction again in the latter
half of the twentieth century'!

Jack: That's quite possible.

AN EXAMPLE OF A SERVICE OF PENANCE[1]
Of necessity, the printing of the following service will
give the appearance of something rather rigidly struc-
tured. One would hope that in actuality it would be
much more informal, spontaneous, and homely.

Priest: Welcome to you all to this short service of
Penance. We are all members of God's big Family –
His Church. In the past few weeks and months since
we last met, there won't be one of us here who
hasn't done wrong. In doing wrong we have turned
away from God our Father. He didn't turn away from
us. He is not angry with us. Nor annoyed. He is
always loving us, always faithful to us, while we've
been faithless to him. Well, now we have turned back
to him.

Our wrong-doing will have damaged the well-being
of God's Family. And so at the service we are going
to express our sorrow not only towards our Father
but towards each other.

[1] Some prefer the title 'Service of Penance' to 'Service of
Sorrow' in case the latter should lead people to think that tears
would be shed. However, 'Penance' might equally imply that
sackcloth has to be worn. Possibly 'Service of Reconciliation'
might be the best title.

This is what we are going to do tonight: we are going to begin with a hymn.[2] This will put us in the right mood. Then a prayer. After that we are going to have a few short readings from God's book, the Bible. After each reading we're going to pause just for a minute to allow the Spirit of God to speak to us. Then we are going to look over together the ways in which we may have failed our Father and our brothers and sisters in God's Family. After this we will tell God our Father we are sorry. Then just before Fr X and I go into the confessionals for the benefit of those who want sacramental absolution – we will expose the Blessed Sacrament. And when the confessions are over we will finish with a short Benediction.

Hymn

Prayer

Priest: O God our Father we have come together tonight in a spirit of sorrow. You called us to be your sons and daughters and we have not always behaved as your true children should. Our Lord Jesus Christ, our Friend and Brother, we ask tonight to be united to you because only if we are in you can we be reconciled with your Father and our Father. Holy Spirit, we know that if we are to be truly sorry, it will be because of the power to repent that you give us. If we are to change our lives it will be because you will lead us to do so. We want to be open to you always but especially so during this service.

All: Glory be to the Father . . .

[2] Titles of hymns are not suggested as congregations' tastes and abilities vary so widely.

Readings: Sometimes these selections could be read against a quiet background of recorded tranquil music (e.g. 'Pines of Rome' by Respighi.)

Matthew 5:1-16

John 21:9-17

Luke 22:54-62

REVIEW OF LIFE

1st Reader: Let's think first of our relationship with God our Father,

His Son and the Spirit.

Have we talked to God as a Father? (*Pause*)

Have we trusted in his love for us?

Have we believed that his Son Jesus is truly our brother, alive and with us in our daily lives?

Have we listened to his Spirit?

Priest: For the times when we have failed,

(*The response to each*:

All: God our Father, we are sorry, please forgive us.)

2nd Reader: Let's look now at our relationship with our family.

Have we tried to bring happiness into our home?

Have we tried to show equal love to all members of our families?

Have we tried to live true to our vows of Christian marriage?

(*Response as above*)

3rd Reader: Let's look now at our relationship with our friends, our colleagues at work.

Have we forgiven those who have hurt us?

Have we been prejudiced against people of a different class or colour?

Have we done our fair share of work?

Have we been honest in our dealings with others?

Have we put aside part of our income to help those

who are less fortunate?

Have we tried to do the work of the Spirit by bringing people together?[3]

(*Response as above*)

All: I confess. (As at Mass)

Priest: May almighty God have mercy on us . . . (As at
Mass) Let us now offer each other the sign of peace.
(As at Mass)

Hymn

Prayer of St Francis

All: Lord make me an instrument of Your peace.
       Where there is hatred, let me sow love.
       Where there is injury, pardon,
       Where there is doubt, faith,
       Where there is despair, hope,
       Where there is darkness, light, and
       Where there is sadness, joy.
       O Divine Master, grant that
       I may not so much seek
       To be consoled, as to console;
       To be understood, as to understand;
       To be loved, as to love;
       For it is in giving that we receive;
       It is in pardoning that we are pardoned,
       And it is in dying that
       We are born to eternal life.

(A hymn follows while the Blessed Sacrament is ex-
posed. Private confession for those who wish. The
service ends with Benediction.)

[3] Obviously one can offer only a few suggestions as to ways
in which we may have failed. To suggest every possible sin
would require a weekend.

For discussion

1. Any comments on the remarks of Don and Jack?
2. Are members of the group aware of a changing attitude amongst people towards this sacrament?
3. Have any members of the group taken part in a service of Penance? Reactions.
4. Are you convinced that a service such as the one described above adds a needed ingredient (the community aspect) to the sacrament?
5. 'I don't believe in confessing to another human being. I just tell my sins to God and ask his pardon.' How to respond to this difficulty?

CHAPTER 15

The Heart of the Matter

One sad commentary on the presentation of the Faith which many received as youngsters is this: if you were to ask a hundred average Catholics, 'What is the first thing that you can tell me about the Mass?' seventy or so would very likely say, 'It's a mortal sin to miss it on Sunday.' As someone once tartly put it, 'From the way the Mass has been preached, you would believe that at the Last Supper Jesus was working out just another way in which his followers could commit a mortal sin.'

SOUR REACTION
In the questionnaire referred to earlier in this book – one question asked was 'What do you think of when you hear the words "Roman Catholic Church"?' The answer received was almost totally uniform: 'Having to go to Mass on Sundays.' Some of the pupils (third-year secondary) drew cartoons to match their replies. One, typical of the sour reactions of many, portrayed the priest with arms outstretched saying, 'The Lord be with you.' In the congregation one youth is pointing at the priest and saying, ''Ay mate yer on yer own'!

LAW OR LOVE
Young people today are far less concerned about the law of the Church than their elders. Many people deeply regret this. Regret it or not, it is a fact of life which we have to face. If we are not able soon to replace obedience to the laws of the Church, which is of doubtful

motivation, with a genuine love of the Eucharist, then in ten years' time we shall still have our fine big churches, but they will be almost empty.

If our youngsters do begin to love the Mass, it will almost certainly be due to three influences: (a) the attitude to the Mass of their parents and older brothers and sisters; (b) the attitude and manner of priest and congregation of the church they normally attend; (c) their understanding of what the Mass is all about – in that order of importance.

PARENTS, PRIESTS, TEACHERS

If parents seem to enjoy the Mass, look forward to it, and are happy about it afterwards, then this attitude will very frequently be shared by the children. As we saw earlier, values are 'caught' rather than 'taught'. The best sermon on the Eucharist is the silent one given by the parents' own witness.

If the Mass is celebrated in a dignified yet happy fashion by a priest who says the prayers as though he really means every word – but not dawdling – who appears to welcome his congregation's joining in with him, who is not disconcerted by babies' squawks or the noise of late-comers – the atmosphere of such a Mass and the genuine warmth of the people present – especially if they sing happily and uninhibitedly – can have a tremendous influence on our young people.

Finally, our youngsters must have an understanding of the Mass that goes a little further than 'You've got to go on Sunday.' Further even than 'The priest says the words of consecration and the bread and wine become the body and blood of Christ. Those who want can then go to Communion' – the way one young person put it to me recently.

A MYSTERY

The Mass is a mystery.[1] That does not mean to say that
we cannot understand it. It means this: that although
every year we will grow to appreciate its meaning
more and more, we will never be able to say, 'Now I
understand everything there is to know about the Mass.'

Nor will anyone ever be able to write a complete
explanation of the Mass. The few lines that follow are
merely a few thoughts which the reader may find helpful.

A VERY SPECIAL MEAL

In March every year Jewish families had a special meal
which they looked forward to rather as we look forward to our Christmas dinner. As a young boy, Jesus
would be excited on the Paschal eve because he, like
every boy in a Jewish family, had a special part to play.
After the table had been prepared and special dishes
laid upon it, he had to ask Joseph this question: 'How
is this night different from all other nights? For on all
other nights we may eat either leavened or unleavened
bread, but on this night only unleavened. On all other
nights we may eat other kinds of herb, but on this night
only bitter herbs . . . On all other nights we eat either
sitting upright or reclining, but on this night we all
recline . . .' And Joseph, like the heads of all the other
families in the land, would describe how this meal was
very special indeed.

A NEW LIFE IN A NEW LAND

The meal recalled the two main events in the history of
the Jews: their deliverance by God from slavery in

[1] This paragraph and the subsequent four are taken from
Catholic Prayer Book and reproduced by permission of the
publishers.

Egypt and the agreement made by God with Moses as the representative of the people. This agreement was called the 'Covenant'. The people agreed at Mount Sinai in the desert, to keep God's Commandments: 'All that the Lord has said, that we will do,' they shouted together. Then Moses built an altar and he poured part of the blood of an animal sacrifice over the altar (which represented God) and sprinkled the rest over the people. The Jews thought of blood as the very life of a person. So in this ceremony Moses was making it clear that God was henceforth willing to share his life with them. Moses ended the ceremony by saying these words: 'This is the blood of the Covenant that God has made with you.'

Every year, the Jews at this Paschal meal not only thanked God for saving them and renewed their Covenant with him, they relived this experience of the past and joined themselves to Moses and his people on this march to a new life in a new land.

DURING SUPPER

The last meal Jesus had with his apostles before he died was this Paschal meal. But a Paschal meal in which this ancient ceremony was changed greatly. Perhaps the meal began in the normal way with John, the youngest present, putting the traditional questions to Jesus as the 'father' of the family. But then, later, as Jesus took the bread and broke it, he told them that this was his body which would be sacrificed for them. And as he passed the cup to them he said, 'this is my blood, which seals God's covenant, my blood poured out for many for the forgiveness of sins.' (Matthew 26:28) The apostles would immediately remember the words Moses had said when he and his followers ratified the agreement made between God and themselves. They would see that Jesus was making a new Covenant with his Father.

In all the houses of Jerusalem the people were taking part in a Paschal meal 'in memory of Moses'. Jesus said, 'Do this in memory of *me*.' In all the other Paschal meals the people were expressing their willingness to abide by the Ten Commandments. But Jesus went further, 'I give you a new commandment: love one another; just as I have loved you, you must love one another.' (John 15:12) Later on he repeated the same commandment: 'This is my commandment; love one another as I have loved you.' (John 15:17)

WHAT WE DO AT MASS

This then is what we do at Mass. We not only thank God for sending Jesus to save us from slavery to sin, we give ourselves to the Father, with Jesus. We say, 'This is my body and my blood – my whole life offered with the sacrifice Jesus made of his whole life to the Father.' We especially make the Sunday Mass an expression of the way we have tried to live in friendship with others during the week. If I am hurting others in any way, or keeping people apart, then my partaking of this meal is a mockery, a pretence. You remember Jesus' words, 'If your brother has anything against you, leave your gift on the altar and first go and be reconciled.' (Matthew 5:24) It's for this reason that we offer each other the 'sign of peace' at Mass.

We say that the Eucharist is Memorial, Sacrifice, Sacrament (or meal), and Presence. As we look at the meaning of each word, we must remember that the four ideas are really inseparably linked. However, there seems no other way of understanding them but by looking at them separately.

1. MEMORIAL

The best understanding of the meaning of this word 'memorial' comes from the actual words of the Eucharistic prayers:

'Do this in *memory* of me.'

'We *recall* his passion, his resurrection from the dead and his ascension . . .'

'In *memory* of his death and resurrection . . .'

'Father, *calling to mind* the death your Son endured for our salvation, his glorious resurrection and ascension . . .'

'Father, we now celebrate this *memorial* of our redemption.

We *recall* Christ's death, his descent among the dead, his resurrection, and his ascension to your right hand . . .'

We recall these saving events in the life of Jesus Christ. At the same time we recall THE saving event in our own lives – our Baptism. We are recalling in the Eucharist not only the death and resurrection of Jesus, but our 'death' in the font and the new life to which we arose. We say: Christ *has* died, Christ *is* risen, Christ *will* come again. In a similar way: We *were* baptized. We *are* Christ-ened. So we *will* meet him when he comes again.

2. OUR SACRIFICE

By our baptism, then, we were buried with him and shared his death, in order that, just as Christ was raised from death by the glorious power of the Father, so also we might live a new life. For if we become one with him in dying as he did, in the same way we shall be one with him by being raised to life as he was. (Romans 6:4-5)

In ordinary speech sacrifice means GIVING AT A COST TO

ONESELF. Jesus' sacrifice was not just at the moment of his death. His whole life was sacrificial. His death/ resurrection was the climax. At Mass, he is made present for us in that same mode of self-offering. But we cannot be 'content to offer a sacrifice exterior to ourselves . . . Since Christ's sacrifice consists in Christ's dying and being glorified in God, we can offer it only by dying and rising in Christ. One cannot therefore be a genuine celebrant of the Eucharist without a communion in Christ and a personal involvement in his redeeming mystery. Apart from that, the lay Christian can certainly perform the gestures of the [Mass]; the priest can even be the instrument whereby Christ makes himself present to his Church and offers himself in her. But if they are not personally associated in the redemptive act . . . then the Mass will not be their sacrifice . . . they will be like the priests of the Old Testament who offered a victim external to themselves . . . they will not be offering the Christian sacrifice.'[2]

We bring the sacrifice of our daily living – the exasperations, the abrasive tensions, the humiliations, the occasional generosities, and unite them with the once-for-all sacrifice of Christ made contemporaneous with our own lives today through the Eucharist.

3. UNION IN A MEAL

When Jesus said the words, 'This is my body which will be given up for you.' 'This is the cup of my blood' – his meaning is clear: 'THIS IS ME.' In our Communion (literally, 'union with') we put the seal on our willingness to offer ourselves with him in sacrifice.

In Jesus' sermon on the Eucharist, (John 6) the words,

[2] From *In the Redeeming Christ* by F. X. Durrwell (Sheed and Ward, 1963), p. 76.

LIFE, LIVING, LIVE, appear 22 times. So our communion is not only a pledge from us to him of our willingness to offer ourselves in sacrifice, with him; it is also a pledge from him to us, that we will have life here and now and life after bodily death – a life without any end . . . 'I will raise him up on the last day . . .' (he uses this phrase three times). 'The one who eats this bread will live for ever.'

This meal unites us not only to Jesus Christ, it unites us to each other. It's not just 'Jesus and me' at Communion. It's 'Jesus and us'. We are God's family around the Father's table. 'Because there is the one bread, all of us, though many, are one body, because we all share the same loaf.' (1 Corinthians 10:17) After Communion I should not put shutters up around myself to cut off the rest of the congregation, any more than at a family celebration, an individual can eat his share of the feast on his own in the box room.

4. PRESENCE

There are many 'presences' of Jesus Christ.

When you leave your house for church on a Sunday morning, Christ is present to you, living in you. This is what we mean by the phrase 'state of Grace' . . . 'My Father and I will come to him and live with him.' (John 14:23)

You enter your local church and members of the congregation have already arrived. Jesus said, 'where two or three come together in my name, I am there with them.' (Matthew 18:20) There is no 'as it were', or 'in a maner of speaking' in his words: 'I am there.' He is *really* present among Christians who gather in his name.

During the Eucharist, the Bible is read. 'He is *present*

in his word, since it is He himself who speaks when the Scriptures are read in the Church.'[8]

Through the power of the Spirit, Jesus Christ becomes present in the Eucharistic prayer as we commemorate what he said and did at the Last Supper. This presence is called 'Sacramental'.

It is a presence unlike the presence of a person located in a room. It is a presence outside our experience, but accepted through our faith in the word of Christ. Though we have traditionally spoken of this as the 'Real Presence', it would be sad if that were to lead people to think that the other presences were 'unreal'.

LINES OF COMMUNICATION

How are people present to each other? The silent passengers in a bus are physically present to each other, but this is surely a minimal presence – merely one in which they happen to be thrown together for a while in bodily proximity. The astronauts in sky-lab in daily communication with their wives are much more present to their spouses than the passengers on a bus are to each other. For they acknowledge each other with interest and love. They communicate. Presence consists almost entirely in communication between persons. If they do not communicate, they can hardly be said to be present to each other. So it is with Jesus Christ and ourselves. He is present in all these different ways, and while my faith in him does not cause his presence, it is only by faith that my eyes will be opened to 'see' him there.

For discussion

1. Have members of the group any experiences they would like to share about their own or their chil-

[8] Decree on the Liturgy, art. 7.

dren's liking the Mass or their finding it a burden-some duty. Practical suggestions?

2. What is the relationship between 'We are baptized' and 'We celebrate the Eucharist'?

3. How is the Eucharist linked to our daily lives?

4. Any suggestions as to how we pray in the silent time after Communion?

CHAPTER 16

Talking, Listening and Just Being Quiet

The priest was trying to explain to the children how praying need not mean reciting prayers by heart. 'Just imagine,' he said, 'that Jesus came back again to our neighbourhood just as he was in Palestine and that he decided to visit this school. Tuesday next is the day fixed for his visit. Naturally we are all very excited. All the more so when we hear that he is not just going to come round the classrooms; he wants to have a chat with each pupil, privately, on his own.

'On Tuesday morning while everyone is in class, Mr Vincent, the headteacher, meets Jesus at the door. He has a chat with him first. Then the pupils start one by one to go into his room for the interview. Eventually it is your turn. As you approach the room you feel perhaps a little nervous, but more likely excited. You say to yourself, "I'll never have another chance like this." You think of all the people whose lives he has changed; who after meeting him discovered just how happy and wonderful life could be. You wonder if your meeting with him and your conversation with him can do the same for you.

'You knock at the door, gently. A kindly voice says, "Come in." You open the door, and there he is sitting in an easy chair. An empty chair is opposite to him and you sit down in it. You look at him. He looks at you and smiles. Now what are you going to say?' Here the priest paused to give the children time to think. 'Are you going to mumble rather quickly, "Our Father, who

*art in heaven, hallowed be thy name . . ." I don't think
so.' The children laughed heartily at the thought of
such an absurdity. 'Still less are you likely to say, "Hail
Mary, full of grace . . ."*

'Now don't get me wrong. Both those prayers are
very good. But they are meant mainly for when we are
praying together in common. When we are talking
with God our Father, or with Jesus, our Brother, on our
own, privately, generally the thing to do is to use your
own words – and not other people's.'

Of course, there is no best way of praying. 'We have to
pray as we can, not as we can't,' is a useful guide. If the
Rosary or the repetition of the Jesus Prayer leads you
into close contact with God, then it is good. If you
want simply to be quiet in his presence then that's good
too.

But person-to-person contact with the Father is the
aim. If two people are in love, they are very much
aware of each other's presence. They speak to each
other and enjoy their conversation. They listen to each
other and try not to miss a syllable or a nuance of
meaning. Sometimes they are quiet in each other's company, confident that they need not be always speaking.
In fact the more in love they are the less the need for
words.

LISTENING COMES FIRST

It's easy to think that praying means, first of all, talking to God. That when I decide to pray, it's as though I
am taking the initiative and that God will begin to
listen to me when I start to speak to him. In fact, it's
the other way round: God always takes the initiative.
It is I who respond. When I begin to pray, I open
myself to his overwhelming presence.

Archbishop Bloom has a wonderful passage on this
subject of 'listening'.[1] He tells of an old lady who came
to seek his advice just after he had been ordained. She
put her problem thus:

'These fourteen years I have been praying the
Jesus Prayer almost continually, and never have I
perceived God's presence at all.' So I blundered out
what I thought. I said, 'If you speak all the time, you
don't give God a chance to place a word in.' She
said, 'What shall I do?' I said 'Go to your room after
breakfast, put it right, place your armchair in a
strategic position that will leave behind your back all
the dark corners which are always in an old lady's
room into which things are pushed so as not to be
seen. Light your little lamp before the ikon and first
of all take stock of your room. Just sit, look round,
and try to see where you live, because I am sure that
if you have prayed all these fourteen years it is a
long time since you have seen your room. And then
take your knitting and for fifteen minutes knit before the face of God, but I forbid you to say one word
of prayer. You just knit and try to enjoy the peace
of your room.' She didn't think it was very pious
advice but she took it. After a while she came to see
me and said 'You know, it works.' I said 'What
works, what happens?' because I was very curious
to know how my advice worked. And she said 'I did
just what you advised me to do. I got up, washed, put
my room right, had breakfast, came back, made sure
that nothing was there that would worry me, and
then I settled in my armchair and thought "Oh how
nice, I have fifteen minutes during which I can do
nothing, without being guilty!" and I looked round
and for the first time after years I thought "Goodness

[1] *School for Prayer* (Darton, Longman and Todd, 1970).

what a nice room I live in – a window opening on to the garden, a nice shaped room, enough space for me, the things I have collected for years." ' Then she said, 'I felt so quiet because the room was so peaceful. There was a clock ticking but it didn't disturb the silence, its ticking just underlined the fact that everything was so still and after a while I remembered that I must knit before the face of God, and so I began to knit. And I became more and more aware of the silence. The needles hit the armrest of my chair, the clock was ticking peacefully, there was nothing to bother about, I had no need of straining myself, and then I perceived that this silence was not simply an absence of noise, but that the silence had substance. It was not an absence of something but the presence of something. The silence had a density, a richness, and it began to pervade me. The silence around began to come and meet the silence in me.' And then in the end she said something very beautiful. 'All of a sudden I perceived that the silence was a presence. At the heart of the silence there was Him who is all stillness, all peace, all poise.'

TO THE FATHER

Admittedly, it's not everyone who will have the leisure and time available to this old lady. Nevertheless the point is valid. 'Speak, Lord, for your servant heareth' should be part of every prayer.

In our speaking to God, we will be aware that the desire of Jesus is primarily that we should speak with his Father. In almost every reference to prayer in his sermons (and there are many), he presumes that we will be talking with his Father. Once we are aware of this, while we may well at the start of our prayer have Jesus in our mind, and in our imagination, and indeed, begin to converse with him, we will quickly realize that it is with him and in him that we shall be speaking to the Father – and possibly also using the intimate form of address he used: 'Abba.' It is the Spirit who gives us the power to talk with our Father in this way. 'The proof that you are sons is that God has sent the Spirit of his Son into our hearts: the Spirit that cries, "Abba, Father"' (Galatians 4:6); 'The spirit you received is not the spirit of slaves bringing fear into your lives again; it is the spirit of sons, and it makes us cry out, "Abba, Father!"' (Romans 8:14) (Jerusalem Bible translations)

A FAMILIAR NAME

All the time we are praying we must be aware that we are addressing an intimate 'you'. God our Father is not an 'It' to be kept on the right side of! The next question then is what name have we to address him by? Surely we cannot, in our intimate prayers give him the cold title 'God'; still less, it would seem to me, 'Almighty God'. (Jesus never used the adjective, 'Almighty' of his Father.) 'Lord' is somewhat ambiguous – are we addressing the Father or our Lord?[2] It's not for me even to suggest alternatives to the 'Abba' sanctioned by Scripture, but it would certainly seem that each person should have some intimate form of address.

GENUINENESS

We can't lie to our Father. We must be genuine with him. We must tell him how we really feel in our hearts. Sometimes we may feel angry with him; or disappointed. Sometimes he may not seem to be present. 'The

[2] The English translation of the Mass prayers ('Lord') leads many people wrongly to believe that they are addressing most of their prayers, not to the Father, but to our Lord.

day when God is absent, when He is silent – that is the beginning of prayer. Not when we have a lot to say but when we say to God: "I can't live without you. Why are you so cruel, so silent?" ' (Bloom op. cit.) This speaking to God from our hearts does not imply lack of reverence. A young lover can hold his bride in awe even though his relationship with her is intimate and relaxed. 'I adore you – I worship you,' he says unselfconsciously. So also with God our Father; despite all our intimacy with him, he is all-holiness. We must not think of him simply as 'a man writ large'. This awareness of his supreme greatness is the necessary prelude to ADORATION – perhaps the most basic of prayer-attitudes. The type of prayer that Jesus is described as saying most frequently is THANKSGIVING – and a Christian has been described as one who goes through life thanking God (the meaning of 'Eucharist'). SORROW or repentance is the first call of the Gospel. 'Repent and believe.' ASKING, too, must figure largely in our conversation with our Father. While we should not hesitate to let our needs be known to him, we must be careful not to approach him with 'a shopping list'. Asking 'for other people' rather than 'for things for myself' is a good guide. But always with the proviso – 'Not my will but yours'. We pray not to get God to do what *we* want. Praying should lead us to be prepared to do what *he* wants. In accepting whatever he wants we are demonstrating our TRUST.

SAYING THE SAME THING

Adoration, Thanks, Sorrow, Asking, Trust, should be the constant ingredients of our prayer. Often enough these attitudes will be implicit and not necessarily expressed. In fact, they are all saying the same thing:

I adore you = I depend on you completely

I thank you = I depend on you completely
I am sorry = I depend on you completely
I am asking = I depend on you completely
I trust you = I depend on you completely.

Our total dependence on this loving Father of ours is at the very heart of the Old and New Testament message. It is a refrain that is repeated over and over again. It is a lesson that is very hard to learn.

When we pray we are telling our Father nothing new. When, for example, I say, 'Father, I am not a good son. I really am a sinner,' God does not reply, 'I'm glad you told me that. I wouldn't have known otherwise.'

When we pray, although it is our Father we are addressing, we are also reminding ourselves of the foundation of our relationship – namely, this utter dependence of me on him.

IN THE FAMILY

Mothers and fathers with very young children, once they are convinced of the value of personal, informal listening and talking to God, will want to see this manner of praying become normal routine in the home. If the children enjoy talking to their parents (and they will, if they see that their parents are really listening and not just making affirmative noises such as 'Really!' 'Is that so?' 'Fancy that!'), then there is a good chance that they will see the value of talking with their Father in heaven. If, on the other hand, there is hardly any genuine conversation between child and parent, then it is less likely that there will be any genuine conversation between the child and God. Why should he speak to a Father he cannot see, if he has never known the enjoyment of speaking with a father and a mother he can see? The child may recite formulas – 'to keep on the right side of God' or 'to get what I want'. But neither could be described as very desirable motives for prayer.

HOME AND DRY

A mother, some ten minutes or so after her eleven-year-old went upstairs to bed, passed his bedroom and overheard him praying spontaneously in some such words as these: 'Father, thank you very much for the love you've shown me today in all the care that others have for me. I want to show you that I care for you. I'm sorry, if today I've been a bit mean. I will try hard tomorrow to be kind to everyone I meet. I trust you to help the doctors and nurses get Granny better soon. I'll say goodnight now, Father God.'

She ran downstairs. She said to her husband, 'I've just heard Brian talking with God. He really looks on God as a Father, as someone who is on his side. Don't you think now that as far as Brian is concerned we are home and dry?' This conclusion may have been just a little premature, a little too sanguine. Even so, mothers and fathers who sense that their children have this sort of relationship with God should feel very grateful.

OLDER FAMILIES

What of parents of older children who are aware, some-what regretfully, that there is no family prayer in the home? What can they do? Certainly their difficulties are greater than those of the mothers and fathers of very young children. Selfconsciousness and embarrass-ment can inhibit the start of a habit of praying together at home. The difficulty can be resolved only by the members of the individual family, aware of their own particular way of living together. It might be helpful to have a look at one or two contemporary prayerbooks.[3]

[3] Here are four titles: *The One Who Listens* by Hollings and

In the meanwhile it may be useful to make a start with grace at meal-time. There is nothing wrong with the traditional grace ('Bless us O Lord and these thy gifts . . .') except that it is hackneyed through over-use. Why not ring the changes?

Father, bless us as we eat this food together in friendship.

Father, thank you for the love and care which you show us through the good meal we are going to eat together. We make this prayer to you through Jesus Christ, our Lord.

Father, as we eat this meal together in the comfort of our homes, may we be mindful of those who are lonely, or hungry or who feel they are uncared for. May your Spirit console them. We pray to you in the name of your Son Jesus Christ.

Perhaps members of the family could take it in turns to make spontaneous prayers such as this. Indeed, meal-time may be the only occasion when the family has the opportunity of praying together.

For discussion

1. Are the members of the group able to offer each other suggestions based on personal experience which may be helpful: (a) as regards private, personal prayer, (b) as regards family prayer.

2. What of the mother's assessment of Brian's relationship with God? What influences would have led Brian to speak to God in this manner?

3. The juniors were going to camp on Tuesday. On the previous Sunday the priest had prayed for rain – the

Gullick (Mayhew-McCrimmon, 1972); *Catholic Prayer Book* by A. Bullen (Darton, Longman and Todd, 1970); *The Daily Prayer Book* by Harold Winstone (Mayhew-McCrimmon, 1971); *A Christian's Prayerbook* by Peter Coughlan (Geoffrey Chapman, 1972).

cabbages recently planted in this farming area were dying off for lack of water. On the Monday the children prayed for a rainless ten days. What about this sort of situation?

4. Anne said, 'I don't talk to God any more. I haven't excluded him from my life. It's just that I can't talk to him the way I used to. But I am aware of his presence close to me almost all the time.' What about this view of prayer?

CHAPTER 17

Understanding Sexuality[1]

'But why should we now have to get all excited about sex education? We never had it when we were children. We were told nothing . . .'

The reason why educators are becoming more and more concerned that a child should be given the right information about, and the right attitude towards, sex as early in his life as possible is that otherwise he is certain to be given wrong information and wrong attitudes. Pressures from the mass media have increased enormously since teachers and parents were themselves children; sex is treated quite openly in newspapers, magazines, books, radio, television, films, advertising. All those sources have brainwashed many children into a false and dangerous understanding of sex. Attitudes are formed which are often opposed to the Christian concept of love, sex, marriage, virginity and family life.

YOUR CHILD'S HAPPINESS

The document on Education of Vatican II says that 'with the help of advances in psychology and in the art of science teaching, children and young people should be assisted in the harmonious development of their physical, moral and intellectual endowments. As they advance in years they should be given positive and prudent sexual education.' What is at stake is the child's

[1] Some of this chapter is taken from my previous book, *Parents, Children and God* (Fontana, 1972); and based upon notes prepared by the Educational Subcommittee of the Liverpool Catholic Marriage Advisory Council. Reproduced with permission.

happiness. If he does not receive the right sort of help, he is likely to grow up with a warped attitude towards sex. This could inhibit his moral development during adolescence. Even the happiness of his eventual marriage might be affected.

A GRADUAL PROCESS

Sex education is the development of correct attitudes concerning love, marriage and family life. This cannot be achieved without giving information about the various sexual organs and their functions. This educational process is a gradual one starting in infancy and developing right through childhood, adolescence and adulthood. The developing child needs enlightenment and guidance to enable him to grow to maturity in chastity. There will be need for much repetition and a growing vocabulary suited to the age of the child. He needs to experience love and security in order to develop correct loving relationships as he matures. The importance of parents providing such an environment cannot be overstressed. The love of father and mother is basic. The school, as an extension of the family, will reflect this love in its attitudes to the children entrusted to it.

A GOOD HOME

The most important of all the influences contributing to the sex education of children is the family. Nothing can replace the influence of a good home where there is a loving relationship between all members of the family. It is best that a child's first step towards a knowledge of procreation should come in truthful answers to questions in the family setting, for example, when another baby is expected. Good parents, however, often lack confidence, particularly in giving information simply and informally. But they can easily find help.

THE ROLE OF SCHOOL

The education of a child from infancy to maturity obviously involves more than the parents. It is not a question of either the school or the parents, but of the school complementing the work of the home rather than acting as substitute. Frequently, however, the home fails to supply what is necessary and rather than leave a gap in the growing child's education, it is the duty of the school – because it is concerned with the whole child – to supply what is lacking. The child will ask questions at school about his own origins which he may not ask at home. Questions may also arise from answers he has received at home or at school. If a child asks a question, whether at home or at school, he is requesting an answer and an answer should be given. Such knowledge is the foundation of an ever-increasing understanding of and response to the mystery of God, creation and life. Human sexuality is good, and a right understanding of it is necessarily good too. Children must grow to an understanding of this gift of God and its purpose in God's love for the world he created.

ANSWERING QUESTIONS

It is important that questions about sexuality should be dealt with both at home and in school. Answers must always be truthful, suitable to the age and maturity of the child and sufficient to satisfy his curiosity. Parent and teacher should be able to answer these questions. It would be harmful if they gave the impression that there was something wrong in asking questions of this kind. The same questions may well be asked again as the child grows older and assimilates more and more the meaning of the answers.

SOME SUGGESTED ANSWERS
  TO QUESTIONS

As children mature at different rates and ages, their young minds work in different ways. Information given at an early age may be completely forgotten – as we well know in other teaching experience – or stored and recalled when needed. Some retelling may therefore be expected.

2-3 Years – Children should be taught to use the proper names of the sexual organs just as they learn to name their nose, or eyes, or ears. A correct vocabulary is most important for all future learning. They can become acquainted with such words as penis, testicles, vagina, navel. Children at this age often ask what their navel is for. Here a mother has an occasion for strengthening the bond of affection between herself and her child by explaining how they were joined to each other inside her before birth and how she fed and protected him till he was big enough to be born.

3-5 Years – When children begin to notice the differences in sex, they should learn that God has made boys in a special way so that one day they may become fathers and so that little girls may become mothers. This information now links the names of the sexual organs with parenthood and this important information is acquired without any emotional involvement.

5-7 Years – Questions will continue to be asked about the sexual organs. The parents' or teacher's knowledge of the child will help to indicate how much more information to give. The organs should be shown to have a definite God-given purpose linked to parenthood. All questions should be answered truthfully and sufficient knowledge given to satisfy the child. An idea of respect and reverence is associated with the important task of one day becoming a father or mother and working with

God to make more happy children.

5-8 Years – Children of these years will be delighted to find out and accept without disturbance the fact that a baby grows within its mother.

Wonder and awe may be experienced if the child is conscious that his mother or a near relative or neighbour is pregnant and that a new life is growing in her womb. The child should perhaps experience the thrill of feeling the movements of the unborn child in later pregnancy. This may well stimulate questions as to how the baby got there and how it will get out.

The word 'womb' will be mentioned – a word the child will be growing familiar with in praying the 'Hail Mary'.

6-9 Years – Children will want to know about the role of the father. They must learn that they are made partly from the mother and partly from the father; that a tiny little seed, called a sperm, passes from the father and joins with a very small egg, called the ovum, inside the mother. They may ask at this stage, 'How does it get there?' and 'How does it get out?' Then they are ready for the next stage.

8-11 Years – This seems to be the stage which presents most problems and embarrassment – how to tell the children about the act of intercourse. Children at this stage are themselves not emotionally involved and will absorb this information as interesting facts which should be related to love, happiness and the family.

'Father and mother belong to each other and love each other very much. Sometimes when they are hugging each other and are very close to each other, usually in bed, they talk about how much they love each other and how much they love you. It is then that the sperm passes from father to mother. The bridge is the penis and the door to the womb is the vagina. If the sperm meets an ovum then a new baby may start to grow inside the womb.'

This is usually sufficient knowledge for the moment. The child has now learned the whole story and the way is clear for him to learn further details without surprise or embarrassment.

It is important that mothers should anticipate the onset of menstruation and prepare their daughters in a practical way. They should be told of the changes going on inside them and be prepared to expect and to accept menstruation. Unless a girl is well prepared, she may well lose her confidence. Better a year too early than a day too late should be the rule here. Information could be given in an answer to a normal question on sex. Teachers and parents will find that the idea of motherhood and of growing up appeals strongly to girls at this age. It is important that enough information and advice is given at this time – about ovulation taking place fourteen to fifteen days before the first day of menstruation and why blood comes out of the birth passage, the vagina. They should know that this is quite normal – a natural process and part of God's plan. Terms such as 'being unwell' should be avoided. Girls should appreciate to whom they can turn for help when any problems arise.

SOME TYPICAL QUESTIONS AND SUGGESTED ANSWERS

5-7 *Years*

Where do babies come from? Everything grows from a tiny seed, whether it is a plant in the garden, a kitten, a puppy or a baby. A new-born helpless little baby has already been alive for nine months, inside its mother in a place called a womb.

How did the baby get there? Inside a woman's body,

near the womb, are two ovaries containing small eggs and, every month or so, a tiny egg, or ovum, leaves an ovary. Every man has sperm in his body and these have the power to give life to the ovum, which then grows into a baby. The father gives the mother the sperm from his own body; the sperm may join the ovum and a baby starts to grow (be conceived) inside the mother's body.

How does it get out? The mother has an opening between her legs called the birth passage (the vagina) and when the baby is ready to be born it pushes its way down the passage from the womb. The opening stretches and the baby comes out.

Can men have babies? No. Only women have babies. They have a womb where the baby grows. Mothers have breasts so that when the baby is born it can be fed on her milk until it is strong enough to eat food.

Why are boys and girls different? A little girl is made so that she can have babies when she grows up. Inside her body she has two ovaries full of eggs and a place called a womb where the baby will grow when she is married to her loving husband. A little boy is made so that he can become a father when he is a man. The parts of his body which help him to do his share in making the baby are outside his body. The little seed bags are called testicles. The part called the penis which normally passes water can also be placed in the vagina of his wife when he grows up and passes the sperm into her vagina. If the sperm meets an ovum then a baby will begin to grow.

Why does the mother have to go to bed (to hospital) when the baby comes? Because it is quite hard work for the mother when the baby is being born. She gets very tired and often needs the help of a doctor or a nurse to make sure that the new baby is born quite safely.

7-9 Years

Similar questions will be asked at this stage and may be answered in a way suited to the age.

Here is a suggested way of talking to a child of this age, or younger – perhaps to the child who does not ask questions.

'You have surely wondered where little children come from and how God gives them their lives. Well, right at the beginning you were so small that you could not live out here. You were as small as a pinhead. So God made sure you were quite safe and let you grow inside Mother in a special place called the womb. How did you get there? Well, just listen. What do we do when we love each other? We hug and kiss each other. Fathers and mothers love each other very much and hug and kiss too. When they hold each other closely in a special way, usually in bed, so that the penis of the father fits into the vagina of the mother, the sperm from the father may meet an ovum. Then a little baby can come from this. God made it that way. Then he lets it grow inside the mother's body. She protects him there till after nine months he is big enough to live safely out here in the world. When you were big enough you came out through an opening that Mummy has between her legs – down the birth passage called the vagina. Now Father and Mother have always looked after you and love you very much and always gave you what you needed. And they keep on taking care of you and loving you. That is how beautiful God has made it for us all.

'You may meet children who do not know how beautiful all this is. They may talk in a nasty way about men and women having babies. It's just that they don't know how beautiful God has made it. Don't take any notice of that kind of talk. And if you hear them saying things you don't understand, then ask me about it.'

9-11 Years

It is possible that children of this age will ask – for the first time, or again – the basic question, 'Where do babies come from?' Information given should contain all the facts given to younger children, but with more detail.

At this stage, too, there would be questions about the purpose of menstruation and what it entails. This information should be given in good time and before the onset of menstruation. Such opportunity may come from an ordinary question concerning sex.

In the latter years of the junior school, boys and girls need to know about each other. Boys should know that girls menstruate and that temporary physical limitations may result, for instance, in girls wanting to be excused from P.E. or games or swimming.

The Adolescent

One must hopefully presume that the adolescent has received the information given earlier in this chapter. He or she[2] knows the biological facts: sexual differences, intercourse, conception, birth of the baby and so on. So there should rarely be a question of having to give the adolescent further factual information. He is, in any case, unlikely to ask for it since he would be embarrassed to give the impression that he did not fully understand everything there is to know about sex!

However he may hide it, the adolescent does, in fact, have a great anxiety about sexuality. He has a natural curiosity, not so much about the physiology of sex, but about the *relationship* between the sexes, and this curio-

[2] We use the word 'he' for the remainder of this passage simply to avoid the clumsiness of 'he or she'.

sity is stimulated by the mass media, especially by the advertisers. He cannot help but be influenced by the implication in much he sees and hears – that 'everybody's doing it'. He sometimes asks himself, 'Am I a freak?' or 'Am I missing out on something?' 'Most people,' says the philosopher Thoreau, 'live lives of quiet desperation.' If ever there were a time of 'quiet desperation' it is that of adolescence. For the adolescent, loneliness is the predominant emotion. Most human beings are to some extent lonely – they feel out of touch, misunderstood, isolated, unable to communicate, or reluctant to communicate because they don't know anyone who will listen to them. No one suffers from this predicament more than the adolescent. What he would like above all else would be someone mature in whom he could genuinely confide, ask questions of without blushing. It is rare for adolescent boys and girls to establish this type of *rapport* with their parents, although if the parents have talked with and listened to their children from infancy in the way described elsewhere in this book, confidences should be exchanged with greater ease.

In the Christian home there may well be a great reserve in talking about sexual matters, and the adolescent could receive the impression implied by the area of silence surrounding the subject, that sex is something 'dirty', 'undesirable'. 'We don't talk about that sort of nasty thing in this house.' It is hard for older parents whose marriage (one hopes) provides them with sexual joy and satisfaction, to appreciate the sexual insecurity and anxiety of the adolescent. What he needs to hear is that sexual desire is not confined to the kinky characters of television dramas, but that all men and all women, with very few exceptions, still have or once had (probably the former) strong sexual longings. This is a sign that one is alive and human; one may rejoice at the possession of those feelings, not regret them.

Chastity is that virtue which, in the Christian tradition, guides us in the wise use of the sexual dimension of our personality. It is not, despite what some puritan fanatics say to the contrary, a virtue which turns Christians into a third sex who know not desire or passion. It does not make us angels who are unaware of our own bodies or the bodies of others. It ought not even to make us think that the spontaneous sexual urges which are so much a part of our life are either dirty or irresistible temptations. Chastity, rather, is that virtue which enables us to channel our sexual energies in such a way that they enrich and reinforce an open, trusting, and loving human life.[3]

Granted that adolescents have this positive view of chastity, there is more likelihood of them accepting with comparative tranquillity the rhythm of sexual demands. This varies between the sexes. 'With boys there is usually a period in the middle or second half of adolescence when sexual demand becomes very acute. For most girls this is a relatively tranquil period but by twenty-one, twenty-two, the girl enters a period of acute sexual demand.'[4]

For discussion

1. Can you recall the sex education you were or were not given? Does this memory lead you to be anxious for your child's sake? Is ignorance the same as innocence?

2. Sexual information should be given to a child naturally as the occasion arises. But what if the child does

[3] *Life for a Wanderer* by Andrew M. Greeley (Image Books, 1971).

[4] 'Psychosexual Development' by E. F. O'Doherty (from *Consecration and Vows*, Gill and Macmillan, 1971).

not ask any questions?

3. Most adolescent boys, some adolescent girls, go through a stage of self-stimulation. How should parents react?

4. Do parents ever cause their children to look upon sex as unclean, evil, nasty? Can modesty in the home ever become so scrupulously observed as to become prudery?

CHAPTER 18

Some Present Difficulties

There seems to be increasing uncertainty about the optimum age for the first reception of the sacraments of Penance, Eucharist and Confirmation.

Let's look at each sacrament separately. For the child to be able to make a fruitful and valid confession, four conditions are necessary:

(1) that he should want to turn to Jesus in this sacrament,

(2) that he should realize the difference between an accident and deliberate wrong-doing,[1]

(3) that he should have some understanding that sin damages his relationship with God,

(4) that he should be able to express himself well enough to the priest without having to depend to any extent on older people telling him what he should say.

The third and fourth conditions are not easily fulfilled by the young child. For example, if Charles hits Vincent and makes his nose bleed, he knows well enough that he has offended Vincent, and Vincent's parents. But

[1] Young children tend to gauge the morality of their acts by the effects they produce, not by the intention or the malice. So for example: a child may by *accident* break a family heirloom; the result will be catastrophic – tears, recriminations, perhaps smacking. The following day he may bring home a toy he has *deliberately stolen* from a younger child. Mother may calmly tell him he has done wrong and he must take the stolen toy back. But there is no great scene. As a result the child will think the accident was a 'terrible sin', the stealing no sin at all.

whether he has realized that hitting Vincent is 'an offence against God' is another matter altogether. His signs of obvious guilt-feelings will be no indication that he has. A puppy caught on the best armchair can look very guilty but can't be said to have sinned.

The last condition (ability to express himself) will depend to some extent not only on the priest's understanding of small children, but also on the relationship that should ideally exist between this particular child and this particular priest.

At what age then should we expect these prerequisites to be present? A general answer, covering all cases, just cannot be given. No two children are the same. Each child must be considered individually. One bishop[2] put it this way: 'The exact time will depend partly on the home and the school and the priest, and partly on the child. I think the child should want to go – because he sees others going, because he knows he has sins, even small ones, because he has been taught and knows that God loves him and the priest loves him and wants him to go. This may be setting a high standard, and it may be expecting a great amount of individual attention and care and knowledge of children, but that is what the child must get. If he cannot get it, there is something seriously wrong.'

READINESS FOR THE EUCHARIST
According to the decree of St Pius X, three simple conditions are necessary:
(1) a rudimentary understanding of the faith,
(2) an ability to distinguish the consecrated elements from ordinary bread,
(3) a genuine desire to receive this sacrament.
Once again, it is impossible to make a general statement

[2] Bishop Birch of Ossory, Ireland.

as to the age at which children fulfil these conditions. Sometimes a child of six could be ready to receive Communion.

What if the child is ready to make his First Communion but not his first confession?

Rome has indicated that the custom of making first confession round about the time of First Communion be maintained though, of course, not making such a confession obligatory. (Confession can only be *obligatory* for Roman Catholics who are guilty of mortal sin.) However, parents may feel that they should not depart from the recommended practice without reason. In this case they may prefer to postpone First Communion.

READINESS FOR CONFIRMATION

Some people are content to see the present practice in the Roman Catholic Church continue, namely that, as and when, the bishop is able to visit a parish, a collection of individuals of all ages is assembled and presented to the bishop to be confirmed. The individuals so assembled will have in common only the fact that they are communicants who have not been confirmed since the bishop's last visit to the parish.

Others are not so happy at this manner of doing things. They would like to see the celebration of the sacrament reserved for older boys and girls, perhaps on the occasion of their leaving school and only after a much more intense preparation. Supporters of this view say that, celebrated in this way, the sacrament could become an occasion for commitment. They point out that in those countries where Christianity has been abandoned, young people seem still to feel the need for some form of ceremony of dedication at this important stage in their lives.

Against this view, however, there is to be considered the danger of using the sacrament as a means of forcing a decision 'for Christ'. Many young people of this age are experiencing difficulties with regard to faith. This is part of the time-table of growth. We should not force the pace. This time-table is of God's arranging, not ours.

But what is Confirmation for? Is it merely the last stage in becoming a full member of the Church? Is it simply a sacrament whereby the Spirit is offered to those who are prepared to be witnesses of Christ? Or is it a sacrament of commitment? Pope Paul wrote as follows: 'In the Sacrament of Confirmation those who have been reborn in Baptism receive the Holy Spirit, the priceless gift by which they are endowed with special strength, and signed with the character of a Sacrament, are more perfectly united with the Church, in word and deed more strongly to spread and defend the faith.'[3]

The Pope does not here seem to be endorsing the view of Confirmation as a sacrament of commitment. However, the last word on this subject has not yet been spoken.

Doesn't it seem as though there is still conflict between the Bible and Science? After all, the idea of evolution, while still not proven, is accepted by almost all scientists today. How do we harmonize scientific truth with religious truth when they seem to contradict each other?

God is truth and truth is one. God is the author both of scientific and religious truth. The creation stories in the book of Genesis were compiled by men who had no

[3] *Divinae Consortium Naturae*, 15 August 1971.

intention of giving a scientific account of the beginning of the universe. They were concerned to express these religious truths:

There is only one God

God made mankind a unity, not a collection of individuals

Everything God made is good

Men and women are of equal dignity

Men and women turned away from God from the beginning

In turning away from God, they brought misery upon themselves and into the world

Our sins add to that misery

When we turn away from God, we hurt ourselves

Without God's help we cannot live good lives.

If these truths had been expressed in that bald and abstract form, they would have meant absolutely nothing to the people for whom they were intended. Instead, the authors and compilers (editing these strands of folklore only 500 years BC and so several thousand million years after life began on earth) chose to use a poetic story form.

God *did* create – though not in the manner described in Genesis. God *still* creates. There *were* first human beings distinct from animals. How many there were or what their names were, we certainly don't know. 'Adam' is a collective noun meaning 'Mankind' (rather as 'John Bull' means 'an Englishman'). 'Eve' means 'life'. Men did turn away from God from the beginning and the effect is with us now. Just look at the headlines in this morning's paper.

ORIGINAL SIN

We understand the Genesis account of 'original sin' in the same sort of way that we understand creation: a poetic story or parable portraying a truth (just as the parables of Jesus portrayed the truth – we don't ask, 'What was the name of the inn at which the good Samaritan put up the man who had been waylaid?'). The two most important elements in the whole complex notion of original sin are, first, that the grace of Christ is more abundant than the sin of mankind, and secondly, the belief that we cannot save ourselves. We depend upon God who saves us through his Son from this condition of sinfulness. Original sin means that we are suffering from a 'cancer'; the condition is operable, thank God, but not by ourselves.

It seems at the moment we have notable differences in the advice being offered to people by the clergy over the most serious matters. At one time, it used to be our boast that there was complete unity of belief and of moral teaching in our Church. Those days seem to have gone for ever.

Let's look at BELIEF first. There can be no doubt that, since Vatican II, the Church's understanding of many doctrines has developed dramatically. One might list the areas of development as follows: the meaning of Revelation, the collegiality of bishops, the Resurrection, the Church as a community in continual need of self-reform, the relationship of the Roman Catholic Church with other Christian denominations, freedom of conscience, the Eucharist. Some of the clergy, through study, reading, attending courses, have 'kept up with the Church'. Others, for one reason or another, have not. Their understanding, and therefore their preaching of the faith, is still that of the theology textbooks published in the first half of this century. Consequently it is possible to hear in the same parochial church from two priests two sermons on the same subject that might well give entirely different presentations.

Now a look at MORAL TEACHING. Here again, there is a considerable difference of approach between the pre- and post-Vatican way of thinking. The pre-consiliar thinking was to some extent legalistic. As an illustration of what I mean, here is a short extract from a moral theology textbook published in 1941. It deals with the law of fasting.

> The one full meal may not be so interrupted as to develop into two meals. An interruption of little more than half an hour would be contrary to the spirit of the law, unless a faster were obliged for a good reason to interrupt his meal . . . readers and servers at table may take some food before their dinner to enable them to read or serve, for this amount is part of their dinner. So too, if one has risen from table, it is permitted to return shortly after, if some dessert is later put on the table . . . It appears that eight ounces of dry oatmeal may be taken as porridge, though when cooked its weight would be very considerable. The addition of water does not change the nature of the uncooked meal.[4]

Yes, I know that this is an extreme example. I am not trying to prove that theologians of a generation ago confined themselves to this sort of casuistry. I do contend, however, that this example illustrates something of the more legalistic outlook of those years.

Post-Vatican II moral thinking allows LOVE a greater part in dictating the sort of response we make to the

---

[4] While priests of the author's generation were studying this sort of theology, people were then, as today, dying of starvation. 'How terrible for you, teachers of the Law . . . you pay your tithe of dill and mint and cummin and have neglected the weightier matters of the Law – justice, mercy, good faith.' (Matthew 23:23).

Gospel. It also lays much more stress on the dictates of one's own CONSCIENCE. 'Man perceives and acknowledges the imperatives of the divine law through the mediation of conscience. In all his activity, a man is bound to follow his conscience faithfully, in order that he may come to God, for whom he was created.' (Declaration on Religious Freedom of Vatican II)

Some priests today are realizing more than previously that they are not answer-men, with a solution ready-made for every problem. While they will say what they believe the Gospel and the teaching Church have to say on a particular question, ultimately, every man has to decide, using all the gifts and knowledge at his disposal, what, in the sight of God, he believes to be the right course of action in the individual concrete case. He can fool other men. He knows he cannot fool God.

It could be that, whereas in the past, many Catholics have looked to the priest for 'off-the-peg' answers to fit every size and shape of problem, now they are being made to rely more on their own consciences than on the consciences of their confessors.

One gets the impression these days that the Church is falling apart. Looking back ten or fifteen years, things Catholic then seemed to be much more secure. There was little talk of shortage of vocations to the priesthood and religious life. Nowadays, not only are far fewer people offering themselves as priests, brothers and sisters, but the number of those opting out is positively alarming. To give an example, in 1970, for every priest ordained in the United States two men left the priesthood. Things just can't go on at this rate.

One cannot explain away the present unease and turmoil within our Church. Even before Vatican II had ended, pundits were saying, 'After every Council there is a period of great uncertainty. We can expect the same after this Council.' And the pundits were right.

The statement, in effect, says that a few years ago there was a greater sense of security within the Church. I'm sure this is true. We had four hundred years of a consistent policy behind us. The Council of Trent, called in 1545 to deal with the Reformation emergency, had codified laws, fixed the way we taught and learned the faith, settled the way in which, down to the last detail, Mass should be said . . . and much more. We could hardly have imagined a different Church from the pattern Trent had given us.

But a feeling of security can be very near to complacency. Undoubtedly many of us (the author included) had a sense of being right because 'this is the way we've always done it.' We were always in the right. Did we need to reform ourselves? Not us!

As the documents proceeded to emanate from the Vatican Council (1962-65), it gradually dawned on an increasing number of people that what was happening in Rome was really a revolution. If we believe that the Spirit of God guides the Church, then we cannot say, as some have asserted, that this is all one big mistake; that the Church has gone mad.

But it's not only the Vatican Council that has changed our Church. Society too, the whole world, has affected the stance the Church is now beginning to adopt. To take just one example: more and more frequently in society, decisions affecting people are taken only after considerable consultation. To issue peremptory orders from above only provokes insubordination. The authorities in our Church are beginning to learn this lesson.

Then again, the Catholic community is much less ghetto-like than even a decade ago. We are much more open to other sections of society. Undoubtedly, increased mobility, better opportunities for further education, the window on the world provided by television – all this has loosened the ties of allegiance.

According to the statement (in italics above) the feeling of insecurity is further heightened by the critical lack of vocations to the priesthood and religious life. Worse still by the number of priests and religious who are 'asking to be relieved of their duties'. He would be a rash person who would attempt without the help of a truly scientific survey, to analyse the causes of this phenomenon. Most people would agree that if the Church is to continue in a form recognizable to us, it cannot survive without priests, sisters and brothers. One can only be amazed that this critical drop in the numbers of priests and religious (producing a vicious-circle effect) has not stimulated some sort of survey into the causes of it and therefore the remedies indicated.

One feels great sympathy for those who return to the lay state. ('Lay state' is a frightful phrase, but how else describe the non-priestly, non-religious way of life?) They will not have reached this decision lightly for it will almost certainly have involved great personal difficulties. Many ex-priests and ex-sisters and brothers are anxious to continue to be of service within the Church.

Keeping all that in mind, one nevertheless has to admit to a feeling of admiration for the reply of one Catholic priest who was asked if he was going to 'jump ship':

Jumping ship for some may be an act of honesty, courage, protest, necessity, or simply the inability to take any more. For me personally though, it would be an act of weakness, failure, capitulation. I helped sail it in better days; should I give up the ship in a storm? Should I leave it to others with whom I have sailed, to stem the wind, to bail out the water, even to struggle ultimately for survival? I have received too much from this community of faith to be able to leave so easily . . .[5]

For discussion

1. Do members of the group have memories of their own first confession, First Communion, and Confirmation which may point to ways in which parents of today may help their children joyfully celebrate these sacraments?
2. What evidence is there in ourselves and in the world of this 'crack in creation' – original sin?
3. Cardinal Newman wrote: 'If I am obliged to bring religion into after-dinner toasts (which indeed does not seem quite the thing) I shall drink to the Pope, if you please – still to conscience first, and to the Pope afterwards.' Any comments?
4. Is the group divided into: (a) those who look back with nostalgia to the past and wish no changes had taken place in the Church; (b) those who are somewhat impatient at the slowness with which the reforms of Vatican II are being implemented?

[5] From an article in the *Catholic Herald* (17 August 1973).

CHAPTER 19

But What Am I Supposed to Be Doing?

Martin Luther King was assassinated on Thursday, 4 April 1968. It was his untiring work for social justice that brought about his death.

'Do you believe that you will meet a violent death?' he was asked in the last television interview he gave before he was shot.

'I live every day under the threat of death,' he replied. 'I have no illusions about it. I don't think it is important how long you live, but how well you live. I am not concerned about the quantity of my life but the quality. I want to remain busy trying to do a good job for my race, for the human race, for my children and for God.'

What am I, as a Christian, supposed to be doing? It surely cannot be simply a matter of edging my way warily through life, just observing the rules, 'keeping myself to myself', so that at the end 'I shall save my soul and be happy for ever.' There must be more to being a Christian than that.

SQUARE ONE

I believe that a Christian is called, first of all, to *accept himself* with all his limitations. He can do this in the joyful realization that he is redeemed by Jesus Christ, as he actually is, here and now, 'warts and all'. This acceptance of himself is the first base, and the only base, from which he can make any advance. There can be no forward movement, no advance towards human maturity, until a person has begun to understand himself and his emotions, and has accepted them. 'Let me know myself that I may know you, Lord,' said St Augustine, a saying echoed by a contemporary theologian: 'To stand before myself is to stand before God.'

This self-acceptance is the 'square one' to which a person may be forced to go back from time to time. To begin from any other square will mean a false start. This self-understanding and acceptance is by no means easy. Many of us burn up a great number of calories running away from our true selves, expend a great deal of ingenuity in the manufacture of a distorting mirror so that the image we see of ourselves will not be a true reflection.

A MAN FOR OTHERS

A Christian's call is one that will lead him to *feel responsible for others*. Having discovered that he himself is frail, is inadequate, he will be able to identify with the frailties and inadequacies of others. We must 'carry one anothers' burdens,' says St Paul. And Pope Paul, in his closing speech to the Council, said:

> If we remember that behind the face of every man
> – and particularly when tears and suffering have
> made it more transparent – we can and must recognize the face of Christ, and that in the face of Christ
> we can and must recognize the face of the heavenly
> Father, then our humanism becomes Christianity,
> and our Christianity becomes theocentric (God-centred), so that we too can proclaim that to know
> God, one must know man.

The first rule of the famous monastery at Taizé is 'to carry the burden of others, accepting the petty injuries of each day, so as to share concretely in the sufferings of Christ. This is our first discipline.' But I cannot expect this way of looking at life to be other than difficult. It's much more comfortable to insulate myself against the world after the manner portrayed in Jeanette Hind's poem:

> I pull the shade
> Against the rainy street;
> Gas station neon,
> And all stranger feet.
>
> I turn the key
> On scarlet sounds of police
> Collapsing morals and
> Collapsing peace.
>
> Oh I had hoped to be akin
> To Noah with his doves locked in
> But every barricade of doors I plan
> Blows like a futile web . . .
> My family is out there, man![1]

Once involved with other people, I carry not only my own worries, fears, disappointments, doubts. I carry theirs too. This is the result of the affection I feel for them. But the affection must be non-possessive. To love another and not want to possess, to be deeply involved with another without letting the emotional strands of the relationship become entangled, requires considerable maturity and self-discipline, and inevitably involves an element of risk.

TAKING THE RISK
It is a risk that must be taken, for the Christian is one

[1] From *Christian Century* (May 1969).

who will allow Jesus to continue through himself the work of redemption, that is, the work of healing, restoring, forgiving, bringing peace and hope and joy. 'Redemption is not something that happened only two thousand years ago; it is going on now. At this moment the action of God and the action of Christ in his humanity are affecting our humanity. If I am really deeply concerned for others . . . and I am working to change at least a portion of the world in which I live . . . my redemption is actually going on.'[2]

RENEW THE FACE OF THE EARTH

God's first commandment was this: 'Fill the earth and CONQUER IT.' (Genesis 1:28) We are not to sit back and leave the earth the way we found it. We have to transform this world that God has given us. Each of us must leave a mark on the world. At his last supper Jesus prayed for his followers, not that they be taken out of the world, but that they be kept safe from the Evil One who tempts men to abandon the work of redemption. 'I do not ask you, Father, to take them out of the world, but I do ask you to keep them safe from the Evil One.' (John 17:15) Pope Paul has said:

> Our goal must be
> to build a world
> a world developed to the full
> so much so that every man
> no matter what his race or creed
> can live a truly human life.[3]

[2] *Christian Involvement* by Bernard Cooke (Argus Communications, 1966).
[3] *This is Progress* (Catholic Institute for International Relations).

TRANSFORMING LOVE

Fear, harassment, moral or physical force may change a situation, but never lastingly for the better. ONLY LOVE CAN CHANGE A SITUATION FOR THE BETTER. The first fount of love is in *marriage* and the home, since the family is the basic cell of human society. The vocation of most Christians will be towards the building up of this family love. Unselfish love in the family will spread outwards and affect others in the community. Love in the community will spill over into the life of the nation: the nation will affect the world.

Other Christians are called by God to the *single state* which by its very nature allows them greater freedom to dedicate themselves and their professional skills to the service of the world. This is, in every sense, as genuine a vocation as that of marriage or the religious life, even though in the past it may have been given scant recognition.

A minority of Christians are called to service in the *priesthood* or *the religious life*. The call demands that a person either leaves home or puts aside the prospect (in the Roman Catholic Church) of ever making a home (a natural and strong instinct), and, to some extent, the right to decide the future pattern of his life. For a person called to community living, the vocation normally includes the vow not to possess anything for himself.

The call to the priestly or religious life undoubtedly demands great sacrifice, but there can be no question of priests and religious regarding themselves as an élitist group, having a 'higher' vocation.

The three callings, married life, the single state, the priest-religious vocation are all complementary.

There are different kinds of spiritual gifts, but the same Spirit gives them. There are different ways of serving, but the same Lord is served. There are different abilities to perform service, but the same God gives ability to everyone for their service. The Spirit's presence is shown in some way in each one, for the good of all . . . Christ is like a single body, which has many parts; it is still one body, even though it is made up of different parts. In the same way, all of us, Jews and Gentiles, slaves and free men, have been baptized into the one body by the same Spirit . . . (1 Corinthians 12:4-7, 12-13)

YOU DID IT FOR ME

'The same Lord is served' by all Christians, no matter which vocation they follow. But how do we serve the Lord today? Jesus gives the answer clearly enough:

I was hungry and you fed me,
thirsty and you gave me drink;
I was a stranger and you received me in your homes,
naked and you clothed me;
I was sick and you took care of me,
in prison and you visited me . . .
I tell you, indeed, whenever you did this
for one of the least important of these brothers of
    mine,
you did it for me! (Matthew 25:35-6, 40)

CHRISTIANS OF THE WORLD, UNITE

The Christian vocation is to one of service. The Christian must be involved with people so as to promote human rights and dignity. In his concern for others, inspired by his intimate relationship with the living Jesus, he will strive for a society which allows people to become real persons. He will be able to achieve very much more if he works with others than if he works on his own. One should expect that those who believe in

Jesus Christ, even though they are members of different denominations, will want to work closely together. Their combined witness to the presence of Christ in the world may help non-Christians to see something of the continuing compassion of Jesus himself. Let's listen to Pope Paul again:

> Christians of every kind
> can work together more and more
> to build a better world,
> a world made human
> by the ending of selfishness and pride;
> a world made human
> by the reign of real fraternal love.[4]

YOU HAVE NOTHING TO LOSE...

It is natural that after years of regarding ourselves as aloof from the other Christian churches, many Roman Catholics should hesitate to join in prayer and work with those who do not share their traditions. But if we are to be in tune with the Church, such hesitations should be put aside. There can be no question of watering down our faith or compromising our beliefs. We recognize that the area of belief common to Christians of all denominations is much larger than the issues that keep them apart. Belief in the Trinity, in Christ, in Christian morality, in the Bible, in baptism, in the Eucharist, in life after death – this and much more is held in common by Christians of all main-stream denominations.

ALL MEN OF GOOD WILL

But it's not just Christians who together should be striving towards building a better world. All men of good will are invited to work together. As Bishop Butler

[4] *This is Progress.*

points out,[5] Pope John was the first Pope in centuries to
address the world, not in the second person plural ('You
people out there are in a pretty bad way') but in the
first person plural. What he said was along these
lines:

> We men, all of us, whatever we believe, or what-
> ever we affect to disbelieve, are all faced in this
> tremendous moment of human history with the most
> enormous problems and with a series of exciting
> challenges; and in that situation, I, in the name of
> Jesus Christ, address myself to all men of good will,
> whatever their creeds, whatever their disbeliefs, and
> what I say to them is this: 'Let us together see what
> we can do, starting if you like from things as they
> are, because it is the situation in its full concreteness
> in which we are all involved, and so pregnant with
> tremendous possibilities. Let us start then with things
> as they are; some, full believers in the Catholic faith,
> others believing in Christ; some believing in God but
> having hesitations about Jesus; others feeling doubt-
> ful about God . . . We've got to see how far we can
> agree on certain principles but, above all, how far we
> can work together in practice.'

Pope Paul in his *Credo* has reaffirmed this outward-look-
ing ideal. The love of God, he has said, 'induces the
Church to promote persistently the true temporal wel-
fare of men . . . to urge them [Church members] to
work to improve their own human conditions within
the limits of their own state of life and possibilities, to
foster justice, peace and brotherhood among men, and
to provide the help that is needed for their poorer and
less fortunate brethren.'

[5] *Christian Commitment in the World* (New Life Publications,
Special issue, Vol. 21, Nos. 5 and 6.

TRANSFORM THE WORLD

This readiness to work with others, no matter what their creed, should not lead us to think that the particular religion to which we owe allegiance is now of no importance. It is simply that we respect the good that is to be found in all people who are sincerely seeking the truth, and we rejoice in the complete liberty of conscience that must be accorded to all men. It is as much a matter of *convergence* as of *conversion*.

Along this road we pray that the Spirit of God, the Spirit who unites, will bring men closer together. In this way the glory of God ('the glory of God is man fully alive') may be made manifest through the transformation of the world.

> After that will come the end, when he [Jesus Christ] hands over the kingdom to God the Father . . . And when everything is subjected to him, then the Son himself will be subject in his turn to the One who subjected all things to him, so that God may be all in all. (1 Corinthians 15:24-28)

For discussion

1. How do you believe we come to a self-awareness and self-acceptance, the 'square one' of all growth towards maturity?
2. If we were involved only with those people who had a right to expect our interest and affection (our family) we could expect a less disturbed life than if we were involved with a wider circle. Why then should we look for trouble by becoming involved with more people?
3. Do Christians of different denominations work and pray together in our area
   at all?
   sufficiently?

In practice, what can we do to increase co-operation between churches?

4. What do you think is meant by 'Christians are called to serve the world'? Are bus-drivers, housewives, traffic wardens, switchboard operators serving the world by their work and thus fulfilling their vocation?

CHAPTER 20

I'll Go On Sweeping the Corridor

This final chapter contains an interview between Mr Roy Trevivian and Beryl. It was first broadcast on 16 June 1968. It should be explained that Beryl was a housewife and a mother. She knew that she had only a short time to live, and it was on the basis of that explicit knowledge that this interview was arranged. Roy Trevivian concluded his introduction to the recording as follows:

'When we had finished the recording, I explained that it wouldn't be broadcast for two or three weeks and she hoped that she would be alive to hear it. I told her that there was no doubt about that – for although she was obviously ill, it didn't look to me as though her death was that close.

'But ten days ago she died and hasn't lived to hear this broadcast. But it is with her agreement and with her husband's permission that we are going to hear now the conversation I had with her three weeks ago. If you are thinking of switching off, because you don't like to think about death, please don't. I think this lady has things to say that will help you.'

R.T.: Do you think it was a good thing for the doctor to tell you that you only had months to live?

Beryl: In my case I am extremely grateful to him. It might not have been the right thing for other people, but it's something that I always wanted the doctors to do for me. When my father was dying we lived out the last six months of his life behind a façade of lies, and it was the most difficult and horrible thing that ever happened to me. I know my father was a great and good man and a splendid Christian, and if the doctor had respected him enough to do for him what he's done for me we shouldn't have had that terrible six months.

R.T.: Now then, here we are, you and I. You know that you are going to die fairly soon and I know this. Can I first ask you about your feelings about death? When you are on your own thinking about 'I am going to die and fairly soon', what then goes on in your mind?

Beryl: Well, you went through the war: were you ever a watchkeeper? That is, have you ever worked all night? Or you're an artist. Have you ever been taken with a perfectly splendid idea and not been able to go to sleep, and you've had to write all night? Or if you've ever been in love and excited and sat at the window and watched the moon go by in the sky. Or if you've been out dancing all night and you've ridden out across the heath and you've come home with the dawn – any of those things. You know what it's like when the darkness comes and the world grows silent and those wonderful hours between two o'clock and four in the morning, when the body is still but the mind is wakeful, and you're aware of truth; and then the darkness goes and the light comes back. And I don't myself, I've never been able to, think of death as anything very different from passing from one day to the next. But that's just me.

R.T.: What's the worst thing about knowing you are going to die very soon?

Beryl: It's not fear of the unknown. It's the anguish of parting from the known and the beloved. I have three teenage children and a husband, and they're pretty well the whole of life. But as a Christian I know that one only dies when God chooses and at no other time, and if he takes me, he will look after them. So it isn't really all that bad.

R.T.: Are you filled with any regret now of time wasted: things you could have done, things you should have done?

Beryl: Oh, yes indeed – but, you see, I've always felt that to sit in the sun and give thanks to God for his glory was just about the best thing. When I was little and at school, the nuns said, 'If you want to find out the value or importance of anything, consider how it will look on your death bed, and say to yourself, "If I'm dead and buried next week, is this important?" ' Well, this was a dangerous thing to say to any school-child, because it gave you a jolly good excuse for not doing your homework. But it was a very good yard-stick, a very good standard of values, when you were looking at your boy-friends or jobs or anything like that. And when I got married and had a family, I had to stop thinking like that, because I should just have sat and played with the babies and not peeled the potatoes or done the washing, you see. And now I wish I had played with the babies more and, you see, just left the things. I've only two regrets: never having prayed enough, never having loved enough.

R.T.: What do you mean when you say 'never having prayed enough', because I'm sure you've been the kind of woman who has prayed a lot?

Beryl: Define prayer.

R.T.: No, you define prayer.

Beryl: Prayer, I was taught, was the raising up of mind and heart to God; and as I grew older I realized that it was the emptying of that still centre of one's being, emptying being of self, and offering it up to God to fill with goodness and Godness; and all action is the overflow of prayer, and any action that is not rooted and based in prayer will come to nothing. And so many actions in my life have not been truly rooted in prayer and have come to nothing.

R.T.: You said you wished you'd loved enough. Now what do you mean by that? You've got a husband and three children and I'm jolly sure, looking at you, that you've been a woman who has loved them. I mean, when you say now that you wished you'd played with the children more, well, only somebody who loves can even see the need for playing with children more. What do you mean when you say you haven't loved enough?

Beryl: Define love. No? All right. Well, I don't think love has anything to do with nice feelings or feeling nice. Love and morality are very, very similar. You look at the crucifix: that is, 'I' crossed out; that symbolizes for any Christian – love. But you remember the crucifix; the crucifixion was not the end of the story – there were two more chapters after Good Friday. There was the glorious surprise in the garden on Easter Sunday and then there was the forty days to the Ascension. Now love in any human beings who call themselves Christians belongs to that, is a part of that, and that's part of their lives. And any one human being, however worthless, was worth the price of the Incarnation, the price of our Lord's thirty-three years on this earth, his Crucifixion, his Resurrection and his Ascension; and next time I feel like saying something mean or petty or unkind, I really ought to stop and think, oughtn't I, the value of the person I'm criticizing?

R.T.: Now let's assume that you have something like a couple of months left to live: how are you going to face these next two months? Is there, are all the moments of the day sort of clouded over by the fact that you're going to die, or what?

Beryl: Now you only ask that question . . . that was a silly question, wasn't it?

R.T.: No, no. I have ministered to people, because I'm a clergyman, who have, up to the moment of dying at any rate, resisted the whole idea of dying and 'Why should this happen to me?' and, you know, 'How unjust of God, if there is a God, to let this happen to me.' I'm wondering how you're reacting to, well, what . . . how are you going to use the last weeks or months of your life?

Beryl: Life is a good gift. It's a tremendous gift, the best gift of all from God; and true life, the life of the spirit, is eternal. It doesn't stop because my body dies. My body is the least important part of me. When the doctor said, 'You're going to die. You'd better come back into hospital.' 'I'm sorry,' I said. 'Well, thanks for telling me. I'm going to latch on to life and I'm not coming back to hospital.' And there was a terrific 'hoo-hah' over this, because they all thought I should go and be a termination case or something. But as I said to you, I think it was St Ignatius who was sweeping the corridor and his novices came and said to him, 'If the world, if you knew the world were going to come to an end in ten minutes, what would you do?' And he said, 'Go on sweeping the corridor.' And that is just what I'm going to do. Only because, I suppose, because I love God and because I believe God loves me . . .

R.T.: You can't persuade me that the knowledge you have got about what is going to happen hasn't either altered your values or high-lighted your values, or convinced you of the unimportance of some things and the great importance of other things. It isn't just a question of going on doing what you were doing before you got this knowledge.

Beryl: No. God doesn't allow you to, because your

physical strength gets less and less. Because I'm very bad at praying and have never prayed much, I reverted to one of my favourite habits as a teenager and before I got married. I allowed myself to go to Mass and Holy Communion every day – that takes perhaps twenty minutes or half an hour. And even if you can't say a single prayer to God, you can lean up against the thought of him, offer your presence there to him as a prayer, and it comes with you for the rest of the day. My husband is the most important person in the world, and has been for the past twenty-odd years, and now it's all that much more important, you see. And my children, but everybody I see – the bus-conductor, the people who serve me in shops, the people you smile at and say 'Good morning' to: they're perfect strangers – you're saying it to God, and perhaps it's God smiling through.

R.T.: What is important to you now that wasn't important to you, or what is unimportant to you now that was important?

Beryl: Well, I can tell you some of the things that are important. I see lots of parents and children – teenagers – and I have the greatest affection for young people, the greatest admiration and respect for their integrity, their virtues, their courage and their generosity. But I feel that grown-ups are so wrapped up in the importance of material living that they get out of touch, you see. And if they'd stop and think: 'Perhaps I may be dead next week, so it really doesn't matter if that poor boy passes his exams or not, or whether he gets a good job or not; but it is important that he should know I, his father, love and respect him and think he's the most wonderful boy in all the world.' And if only parents would say it to their children: 'I respect you, I'm proud of you, I love you.' I think, you know, that children would earn their respect. I'm a terrible coward, and during the war, during air-raids, my teeth used to chatter, and I think for the first ten months of the war I never slept for more than two hours at a time in sheer terror. And I woke up one night – you know, 'The coward in his heart dies many deaths' – and . . . if you face the worst possible thing that can happen to you if you're afraid of something, if you run away that fear will master you, but if you turn round and look at it, go up to it and look at it, either it will change its nature or you find it is some merciful, purposeful lesson of God. And I don't think any of us nowadays make enough allowance for God in our everyday life. Lots of times when you go to church on a Wednesday or a Thursday and you say, 'God, if you want me to feed any more people this week you'll either have to send me the food or the money'; and, believe me, it never fails.

R.T.: Now whenever I think that, or act on that, I always feel it's being rather naïve and superstitious.

Beryl: Well, if you've done everything you can do yourself, I think it's silly not to leave the rest to God. And I think, too, that one should leave it to God before you're absolutely at the end of your tether. You're a father. You wouldn't like it if your son pushed himself to the point of death before he came down and said to you, 'Please help me.' Why do you do that to God?

R.T.: Why don't you expect a miracle? Why have you resigned yourself to the fact that you're going to die? Why don't you say to God, 'God, work a miracle, get me better'?

Beryl: I say to God every day, I say, 'God, I'm going to die when you want me to die, not when the doctors tell me I'm going to.' To me, a miracle is the suspension of the laws of nature, as we know them now. To a lot of my non-Catholic friends, it's answer to prayer, lots of other rather vague and woolly things which I don't really quite understand. But why should God work a miracle for me?

R.T.: But why shouldn't he?

Beryl: Well, if he wants to, he will.

R.T.: And if he doesn't you won't feel hurt, or feel that he has been unkind or unjust?

Beryl: No.

R.T.: I think I know what you mean, because with one's own little children they sometimes ask for something and you can understand them wanting the thing they ask for, but you also know either it is impossible, or else you know it's not good for them.

Beryl: I can see that it could very easily be very bad for my children if they had me round their necks for the next fifty years.

R.T.: I'm sure that's not why God is calling you to heaven – I'm sure that's not the reason – but anyway that's a lovely thing to say. Have you ever had any faint feeling of the injustice of all this? Now one does come across what you might call – now wait a minute – tragic deaths: you know, the young, good, God-fearing, praying, Jesus-loving, young mum who is taken or dies; and then the disillusioned, uncaring person, who's wrecked lives all over the place, goes on living till they're ninety. This does seem a bit odd and unjust, doesn't it?

Beryl: I'm sorry – you're talking a lot of poppycock. This injustice rubbish – who are we to say what is just and what is not just? God is love, God is truth, God is justice. And I'd rather have God's mercy than his justice. And as for the sinner and all that, well, our Lord told us a parable about the labourers in the vineyard

and those who slipped in at the last moment, and St
Augustine: 'Inter pontem et fontem misericordia Dom-
ini.'

R.T.: What does that mean in English?

Beryl: Well, between the bridge and the water, you
know, when the bad old chap fell over, the mercy of
God got him in the very last breath. I don't know anything about justice – I don't really want to – I just want
love and mercy. And some people take longer to work
out their salvation than others. You see, you fight God
when you're young; you fight God, you wrestle with
him till you're black and blue; and then one day he says
just one word in your ear. Nothing's the same again.
The whole meaning of life is changed, isn't it? I think
you know the great psychologists like Jung. They say in
your younger years you're coming to terms with exterior reality and you . . . in your middle years you
withdraw . . . you make this withdrawal and return,
then come to the peak of their lives in their middle
years. And then decline into the grave. But, you see, as a
Christian you've seen the glimmer over the horizon
which gives completely different meaning to the whole
of life. And what is time, what is life?

R.T.: Well now, if you had a glimpse into the meaning of life, what is the meaning of life that you've seen
through your glimmer?

Beryl: Laughter, love and courage and all those old-
fashioned words, which you don't often hear nowadays,
but still have a very, very real meaning.

R.T.: George Harrison, who's one of the Beatles, says
in an article: 'I'm probably going to turn back to
Christianity because I've found in all these other things
that I've looked into that they don't have the answer
I'm looking for. What I want to know is what are we
doing here, what is the meaning of being alive as a

human being?' If you've had a glimpse beyond, what do you think the meaning of being here is for self-conscious, human beings?

Beryl: God made me to know him and love him and serve him in this world and to be happy with him for ever in the next.

R.T.: But that's a straight 'quote' from the Catechism. Now come on . . .

Beryl: But it's part of me – it's what I . . .

R.T.: Put that in your own words.

Beryl: God is . . .

R.T.: Come on, try and make it sense. What is the meaning of being alive, being a human being?

Beryl: When you fall in love you can't talk, you just burble about your beloved; when you write a great poem, sometimes it doesn't come out in words; when you write great music, you can't ask me to say in words all that. God *is*, and we belong to God. And God is all truth, all beauty, and God is love.

R.T.: And are you really saying that the meaning of being a human being is simply knowing and loving God?

Beryl: When the young man says, 'Darling, I love you. Marry me,' and they get married, they're married for life 'till death do us part' – they don't go on saying, 'I love you, I love you, I love you' all this time. They live it. And if . . . This is Christianity, this is living Christ. You're a Christ's man, you have to be other Christs – you have to show forth Christ in your own life and you have to love and serve Christ in others. And you don't do this by thinking it, or by saying it, you do it by being it. And, you see, this is where perhaps – who am I to say? – God, forgive me – where the breakdown has come, 'the scientific development which so far outstripped the philosophical development' – that was said in 1920. Well, which of our old holies has latched on to this, and done something about it? Only the nameless ones, the unknown ones, the ones known to Christ and none others, you see. And I do feel we over . . . give far too much importance to the intellectual side of life and doing. We're intuition, instinct and feeling and, you know, providing you use your brain as you should, you can feel your way to Christ just as valiantly as thinking your way to him.

R.T.: One last question, rather a mundane question, but – and you'll probably be angry with me when I say this – but I've often thought about when my turn comes to die, I would like to kiss my wife and children goodbye, still able to walk, still able to laugh, and say, 'Now, goodbye, cheerio,' and then leave them and disappear. And I've a secret little plan in mind that I will go to a particular place that I know of, a long, long way from them where I would have friends, and I would say, 'Right, I have come here to die, you look after me'; they look after me, I die, but my wife and children – you're laughing at me – but my wife . . .

Beryl: You remind me of an elephant! That's what the elephants do!

R.T.: Well, you say I remind you of an elephant, but because I've felt I don't want those people I love around me when I go a bit peculiar in the head, or go in a coma and all this sort of stuff.

Beryl: Our Lord carried his cross to Calvary – and his mother followed him, and she was the sort of mother who would stand at the foot of the cross when her Son was crucified. And he was the sort of Son who would let her. And what more perfect love and what more perfect understanding could there be than that? And can't you let us do the same? Can't we love each other in that way? In him?

R.T.: So you will want around you those people whom you love most?

Beryl: I haven't really thought about it, but I'll be very glad to leave it to God. For all I know I might drop down dead on the bus amidst strangers. Why worry?

R.T.: Oh, yes, but if you can make plans for it?

Beryl: I think that making plans is very dangerous.